# TOWARD IMAGINATION

# TOWARD IMAGINATION

## CULTURE AND THE INDIVIDUAL

*Seven lectures given in Berlin between June 6 and July 18, 1916*

RUDOLF STEINER

*Translated by Sabine H. Seiler*

ANTHROPOSOPHIC PRESS

This book is a translation of *Weltwesen und Ichheit* (volume 169 in the Collected Works), published by Rudolf Steiner Nachlass-verwaltung, Dornach, Switzerland, 1963.

Published in the United States by Anthroposophic Press



**Library of Congress Cataloging-in-Publication Data**

Steiner, Rudolf, 1861-1925.
[Weltwesen und Ichheit. English]
Toward imagination : culture and the individual / Rudolf Steiner : translated by Sabine H. Seiler.
Translation of: Weltwesen und Ichheit.
"Seven lectures given in Berlin between June 6 and July 18, 1916."
Includes bibliographical references.
ISBN 0-88010-284-5 — ISBN 0-88010-285-3 (pbk.)
1. Anthroposophy. 2. Man. 3. Culture—Philosophy. I. Title.
BP595.S894W45413 1990
299'.935—dc20 90-33835
CIP



Printed in the United States of America

# CONTENTS

# TOWARD IMAGINATION

*During the war, Rudolf Steiner spoke the following commemorative address at the beginning of every lecture he gave to the Anthroposophical Societies of countries affected by the war:*

My dear friends, let us be mindful of the guardian spirits of all those out there on the vast battlefields of the events of our time:

Spirits of your souls, ever working guardians,
May your wings carry
Our souls' imploring love
To those on earth entrusted to your care.
United with your power,
May our prayer be a shining help
To the souls it lovingly seeks.

And turning to the guardian spirits of those who have already passed through the portal of death because of these tragedies:

Spirits of your souls, ever working guardians,
May your wings carry
Our souls' imploring love
To those in the spheres entrusted to your care.
United with your power,
May our prayer be a shining help
To the souls it lovingly seeks.

And may the Spirit whom we have long sought to approach with our spiritual science, the Spirit who passed through the Mystery of Golgotha for the salvation of the earth and for the freedom and progress of humanity, may that Spirit be with you in your arduous tasks.

## LECTURE ONE

June 6, 1916

# THE IMMORTALITY OF THE I

IT WOULD not be fitting to speak of Pentecost in our fateful time in the same way as in earlier days. We are living in a time of severe ordeals, and we cannot look only for the lofty feelings that warm our souls. If we have any right and true feeling at all, we cannot possibly, even for a moment, forget the terrible pain and suffering in our time. It would even be selfish for us to want to forget this pain and suffering and to give ourselves up to contemplations that warm our souls. Therefore it will be more appropriate today to speak of what may be useful in these times—useful insofar as we have to look for the reasons of the great sufferings of our time in our prevailing spiritual condition. As we have found in many of our previous talks here, we have to realize that we must work on the development of our souls particularly in these difficult times so that humanity as a whole can meet better days in the future.

Nevertheless, I would like to begin with some thoughts that can lead us to an understanding of the meaning of Pentecost. In the course of the year there are three important festivals, Christmas, Easter, and Pentecost. Everyone will feel the great difference between them—everyone, that is, whose feelings have not become dulled, as in the case of most of our contemporaries, to the meaning of these festivals in the evolution of humanity and the universe. The difference in our feelings for these festivals is expressed in the external symbolism of the festivities connected with them.

Christmas is pre-eminently celebrated as a festival for the joy of children, a festival that in our times—though not always—includes a Christmas tree, brought into our houses from snow- and ice-clad nature. And we remember the Christmas plays we have performed here on several occasions, plays that have for centuries uplifted even the simplest human hearts, guiding them to the mighty event that came to pass once in the evolution of the earth—the birth of Jesus of Nazareth in Bethlehem. The birth of Jesus of Nazareth is a festival connected almost by nature to a world of feelings that was born out of the Gospel of St. Luke, particularly out of its most popular parts that are easiest to understand. Thus, Christmas is a festival of what is universally human. It is understood, at least to a certain extent, by children and by people who have remained childlike in their hearts, and it brings into these hearts something great and tremendous that is then taken up into consciousness.

Easter, however, although celebrated at the time of nature's awakening, leads us to the gates of death. We can characterize the difference between the two festivals by saying that while there is much that is lovely and speaks to all human hearts in Christmas, there is something infinitely sublime in Easter. To celebrate Easter rightly, our souls must be imbued with something of tremendous sublimity. We are led to the great and sublime idea that the divine being descended to earth, incarnated in a human body, and passed through death. The enigma of death and of the preservation of the eternal life of the soul in death—Easter brings all this before our souls.

We can have deep feelings for these festivals only when we remember what we know through spiritual science. Christmas and the ideas it evokes are closely connected with all the festivals ever celebrated to commemorate the birth of a Savior. Christmas is connected with the Mithras festival, which celebrates the birth of Mithras in a cave. Thus, Christmas is a festival closely linked with nature, as symbolized by the Christmas tree. Even the birth it celebrates is a part of nature. At the same time, because Christmas celebrates the birth of Jesus of Nazareth, which has great significance particularly for us in spiritual science, it includes much that is spiritual. As we have often said, the spirit of the earth awakens in winter and is most active when nature appears to be asleep and frozen. Christmas leads us into elemental nature; the lighting of the Christmas candles should be our symbol of the awakening of the spirit in the darkness of winter, the awakening of the spirit in nature. And if we want to understand the relationship between Christmas and human beings, we have to think of what connects us to nature even when we are spiritually separated from it, as in sleep when our astral body and our I ascend as spirit into the spiritual world. The etheric body, though also spirit, remains bound to the outer, physical body. Elemental nature, which comes to life deep inside the earth when it is shrouded in wintry ice, is present in us primarily in the etheric body.

It is not just a mere analogy, but a profound truth that Christmas also commemorates our etheric, elemental nature, our etheric body, which connects us with what is elemental in nature.

If you consider everything that has been said over many years about the gradual paralyzing and diminishing of humanity's forces, you will be struck by the close relationship between all the forces living in our astral body and the events bringing us this diminishing and death. We have to develop our astral body during life and take in what is spiritual by means of it, and therefore we take into ourselves the seeds of death. It is quite wrong to believe that death is connected with life only outwardly and superficially; there is a most intimate connection between death and life, as I have often pointed out. Our life is the way it is only because we are able to die as we do, and this in turn is connected with the evolution of our astral body.

Again, it is not just an analogy to say that Easter is a symbol of everything related to our astral nature, to that part of our nature through which we leave our physical body when we sleep and enter the spiritual world—the world from which the divine spiritual Being descended who experienced death in the person of Jesus of Nazareth. If I were speaking in a time when the sense for the spiritual was more alive than it is in ours, then what I have just said would quite likely be taken more as reality. However, nowadays it is taken as merely symbolic. People would then realize that the celebration of Christmas and Easter is also intended to remind us of our connection with elemental nature and with the nature that brings spiritual and physical death. In other words, the festivals are tokens reminding us that we bear a spiritual element in our astral and etheric bodies. But in our age these things have been forgotten. They will come to the fore again when people decide to work at understanding such spiritual things.

In addition to the etheric and astral bodies, we bear another spiritual element in us—the I. We know how complex this I is and that it continues from incarnation to incarnation. Its inner forces build the garment, so to speak, that we put on with each new incarnation. We rise from the dead in the I to prepare for a new incarnation. It is the I that makes each of us a unique individual. We can say our etheric body represents in a sense everything birth-like, everything connected with the elemental forces of nature. Our astral body symbolizes what brings death and is connected with the higher spiritual world. And the I represents our continual resurrection in the spirit, our renewed life in the spiritual world, which is neither nature nor the world of the stars but permeates everything.

Just as we can associate Christmas with the etheric body and Easter with the astral body, so Pentecost can be connected with the I. Pentecost represents the immortality of our I; it is a sign of the immortal world of the I, reminding us that we participate not only in the life of nature in general and pass through repeated deaths, but that we are immortal, unique beings who continually rise again from the dead. And how beautifully this is expressed in the elaboration of Christmas, Easter, and Pentecost! Just think, Christmas as we celebrate it is directly connected with earthly events; it follows immediately upon the winter solstice, that is, at the time when the earth is shrouded in deepest darkness.

In a way, our celebration of Christmas follows the laws of the earth: when the nights are longest and the days shortest, when the earth is frozen, we withdraw into ourselves and seek the spiritual insofar as it lives in the earth. Thus Christmas is a festival bound to the spirit of the earth. It reminds us continually that as human beings we belong to the earth, that the spirit had to descend from the heights of the world and take on earthly form to become one of us children of the earth.

On the other hand, Easter is linked to the relationship between sun and moon and is always celebrated on the first

Sunday after the first full moon in spring, that is, the first full moon after the twenty-first day of March. We fix the date of Easter according to the relative position of sun and moon. You see how wonderfully Christmas is connected with the earth and Easter with the cosmos. Christmas reminds us of what is most holy in the earth, and Easter of what is holiest in the heavens.

Our Christian festival of Pentecost is related in a beautiful way to what is above the stars: the universal spiritual fire of the cosmos, individualized and descending in fiery tongues upon the Apostles. This fire is neither of the heavens nor of the earth, neither cosmic nor merely terrestrial, but permeates everything, yet it is individualized and reaches every human being. Pentecost is connected with the whole world! As Christmas belongs to the earth and Easter to the starry heavens, so Pentecost is directly connected to every human being when he or she receives the spark of spiritual life from all the worlds. What all humanity received in the descent of the divine human being to earth is given to each individual in the fiery tongues of Pentecost. The fiery tongues represent what is in us, in the universe, and in the stars. Thus, especially for those who seek the spirit, Pentecost has a special, profound meaning, summoning us again and again to seek anew for the spirit.

I think in our age we have to take these festive thoughts a step further and consider them more deeply than we would at other times. For how we will extricate ourselves from the sorrowful and disheartening events of our times will largely depend on how deeply we can grasp such thoughts. Our souls will have to work their way out of these events. In certain circles people are already beginning to feel that. And I would add that particularly people who are close to spiritual science should increasingly feel this necessity of our times to renew our spiritual life and to rise above materialism. We will overcome materialism only if we have the good will to kindle the flames of the spiritual world within ourselves and to truly celebrate Pentecost inwardly, to take it with inner seriousness.

In our recent talks here we have spoken about how difficult it is for people to find what is right in this area of the renewal of spirituality under the conditions of the present age. We see nowadays a development of forces we cannot admire enough; yet we lack adequate feelings to respond to them. When feelings become as necessary for the spiritual, people will realize that it is important to celebrate and not neglect the inner Pentecost in our soul. Some people—of course, not you, my dear friends, who have after all participated in such studies for several years—might well think our recent talks here smack of hypochondria and carping.[1] I think the very opposite is true, for it seems to me absolutely necessary to point out the things we talked about because people should know where to intervene spiritually in the course of human evolution. In fact, here and there other people also realize what is essential for our times.

The grandson of Schiller, Alexander von Gleichen-Russwurm, has written a nice little book called *Cultural Superstition*.[2] As I read it, I was reminded of many things I said to you here. For instance, I told you that spiritual science should not remain merely a lifeless theory. Instead, it must flow into our souls so that our thinking becomes really enlivened, truly judicious, and flexible, for only then can it get to the heart of the tasks of our age. In this connection, let me read you a few sentences from this booklet *Cultural Superstition* by Alexander von Gleichen-Russwurm.

> If all of us bear part of the guilt for this terrible tragedy, it is because throughout all of Europe, in spite of culture, schools, and other educational facilities, we have gradually forfeited our independent thinking.
>
> O, freedom of thought, in vain have the greatest poets called for you in the name of humanity. You languished, faded—you sank down as if dead! Unfree, we parroted others, our power of thinking chained, lamed, and weary.
>
> We had time, desire, and ambition for everything except actual thinking. Even here, in the erstwhile nation of poets and philosophers, thought has become an illustrious stranger, a rare, disquieting guest. Reading and writing are no longer of any help to us; indeed, they can only be harmful if we do not know how to think.
>
> Recently everything has been conducive to wean us of thinking altogether—everything, even our education, our art, recreation, work, social life, travel, and domestic life.
>
> But genuine culture should teach us above all to think, for feelings and instincts alone will never suffice to make possible a peaceful coexistence of people and nations. For this, a sound, carefully trained, political mind is necessary.

And von Gleichen-Russwurm, this grandson of Schiller, traces the fact that we have forgotten how to think far back in history:

> Since the Vienna Congress of 1815, all nations have made a certain effort to get along and settle down on this planet. Innumerable treaties, attempts of every kind, bear witness to this. People believed that by strug-

gling for a constitution and suffrage they would gain real participation in government and be able to determine their own fate.

Then von Gleichen-Russwurm says we cannot do without thinking. He shows this by painting a strange picture of our present time, which we must always think about and cannot forget even for a moment.

> Indeed, we have not made such wonderful progress when everything that formerly would have been spun into the yarns of the most harebrained poets has become reality. We are in such an immense and frantic jumble, more fantastic than anything that happened during the migration of peoples. Senegalese kill our poets, artists groom horses, professors tend sheep. Theater managers give orders of execution over the telephone, pious Indians seek death on our battlefields in accordance with their ancient rites. Beautiful buildings fall into ruins and shelters fit for cave-dwellers are built. Millionaires starve and struggle with vermin, while beggars sit at abandoned sumptuous tables in old castles. Suspicious characters are rehabilitated and the most harmless people languish and die in prisons.

This state of things compels Schiller's grandson to consider the necessity of enlivening thinking. However, I have not been able to find, either in this pamphlet or in his other writings, that he is looking in the right direction for the true sources of enlivened thinking.

It is indeed not easy to celebrate Pentecost in our soul nowadays, not at all easy. Now I have here the book of a man who has taken great pains in the last few years to understand Goethe—as far as he found it possible—and who has gone to great lengths to understand our spiritual science.[3] This very man, who has really tried to understand Goethe and is delighted that he is now beginning to do so, had earlier written nine novels, fourteen plays, and nine volumes of essays. His case is very characteristic of the difficulties people have nowadays in finding their way to spiritual life. In his latest book, the tenth volume of his essays, he says how glad he is to have found Goethe at last and to have the opportunity to try to understand him. One can see from this tenth volume of essays that the author is really trying very hard to comprehend Goethe. But think what it means that a man who has written so many novels, so many plays, and who is quite well-known, admits now when he is perhaps fifty or fifty-one that he is just beginning to understand Goethe.

Now his latest book is called *Expressionism.* The writer is Hermann Bahr.[4] Hermann Bahr is the man I just described. I haven't counted all his plays; he wrote still more, but he disavows the earlier ones. It is not difficult for me to speak about Bahr because I have known him since his student days; indeed I knew him quite well. You see, he wrote on every kind of subject, and much of his writing is very good. He says of himself that he has been an impressionist all his life, because he was born in the age of impressionism.

Now let us define in a few words what impressionism really is. We will not argue about matters of art, but let us try to understand what people like Hermann Bahr mean by impressionism. Consider the work of artists such as Goethe, Schiller, Shakespeare, Corneille, Racine, Dante—or take whomever you want. You will find that what they considered great about their art was that they had perceived the external world and then worked with it spiritually. In art the perception of the outer world unites with what lives in the spirit. Goethe would have denied the status of "art" to all works that do not strive for such a union of nature and spirit.

But in modern times what is called impressionism has emerged. Hermann Bahr grew up with it and is now aware that he has been an impressionist in all he did. When he discussed paintings—and many of his essays are about painting—he did so from the standpoint of impressionism. When he wrote about painting, he wanted to be an impressionist himself, and that is what he was, and still is in his own way. Now what does such a man mean by impressionism in art? He means by impressionism that the artist is utterly afraid to add anything out of his or her own soul to the external impression given by nature. Nothing must be added by the soul.

Of course, under such conditions no music could be created; but Bahr excluded music. Neither could there be architecture. Music and architecture can therefore never be purely impressionist. However, in painting and in poetry pure impressionism is quite possible. Very well, as far as possible everything coming out of the artist's own soul was to be excluded. Thus, the impressionist painters tried to create a picture of an object before they had properly perceived it, before they had in any way digested the visual impression. In other words, looking at the object, and then right away, if possible, capturing it before one has added anything to the picture and the impression it evoked—that is impressionism! Of course, there are different interpretations of impressionism, but this is its essential nature.

As I said in a public lecture in Berlin, Hermann Bahr is a man who champions whatever he thinks to be right at the moment with the greatest enthusiasm. When he first came to the university in Vienna, he was heart and soul for socialism; he had a passion for it and was the most ardent social democrat you can imagine. One of the plays he now disavows, *The New Humanity*, is written from this socialist standpoint. I think it is out of print now. It has many pages of social democratic speeches that cannot be produced on stage. Then the German National Movement developed in Vienna, and Hermann Bahr became an ardent nationalist and wrote his *Great Sin*, which he now also repudiates. By that time, after having been a socialist and a nationalist, Bahr had reached the age when men in Austria are drafted for military service, and so at nineteen he became a soldier.

He had left behind socialism and nationalism and now became a soldier, a passionate soldier, and developed an entirely military outlook on life. For a year he was a soldier, a one-year volunteer. After this he went for a short time to Berlin. In Berlin he became—well, he did not become a fervent Berliner; he couldn't stand that, so he never became an ardent Berliner. But then he went to Paris where he became an enthusiastic disciple of Maurice Barrès and people of his ilk. He was also an ardent follower of Boulanger who just at that time was playing an important role.[5] Well, I don't want to rake up old stories, and so I will not tell you of the passionate Boulangist letters the enthusiastic Bahr wrote from Paris at that time.

Then he went to Spain, where he became inflamed with enthusiasm for Spanish culture, so much so that he wrote an article against the Sultan of Morocco and his rotten behavior toward Spanish politics. Bahr then returned to Berlin and worked for a while as editor of the journal *Freie Bühne*, but, as I said, he never became an ardent Berliner. Then he went back and gradually discovered Austria. After all, he was born in Linz. Oh, sorry, I didn't mention that before all this he had also been to St. Petersburg where he wrote his book on Russia and became a passionate Russian. Then he returned and discovered Austria, its various regions and cultural history and so on.

Bahr was always brilliant and sometimes even profound. He always tried to convey what he saw by just giving his first impression of it, without having mentally digested it. As you can imagine, it can work quite well to give only the first impression. A socialist—nothing more than the first impression; German nationalist or Boulangist—nothing more than the first impression; Russian, Spaniard, and so on and so forth. And now to be looking at the different aspects of the Austrian national character—doubtlessly an extraordinarily interesting phenomenon! But just imagine: Bahr has now reached the age of fifty, and suddenly expressionism appears on the scene, the very opposite of impressionism.

For many years Hermann Bahr has been lecturing in Danzig. On his way there he always passed through Berlin, but without stopping. He is fond of the people of Danzig and claims that when he speaks to them, they always stimulate him to profound thoughts, something that does not happen in any other German town. Well, the people of Danzig asked him to give a lecture there on expressionism. But just think what that means to Hermann Bahr, who has been an impressionist all his life! And only now does expressionism make its appearance! When he was young and began to be an impressionist, people were far from delighted with impressionist pictures. On the contrary, all the philistines, the petty bourgeois—and of course other people too—considered them mere daubing. This may often have been true, but we will not argue about that now. Hermann Bahr, however, was all aglow and whosoever said anything against an impressionist painting was of course a narrow-minded, reactionary blockhead of the first order who would have nothing unless it was hoary with age and who was completely unable to keep pace with the progress of mankind. That is the sort of thing you could often hear from Hermann Bahr. Many people were blockheads in those days.

There was a certain coffee-house in Vienna, the Café Griensteidl, where such matters were usually settled. It used to be opposite the old Burgtheater on the Michaeler Platz but is now defunct. Karl Kraus, the writer who is also known as "cocky Kraus" and who publishes small books, wrote a pamphlet about this coffee-house, which back in 1848 had Lenau and Anastasius Grün among its illustrious guests.[6] When the building was torn down, Kraus wrote a booklet entitled *Literature Demolished.*[7]

The emergence of impressionism was often the topic of discussion in this coffee-house. As we have seen, Hermann Bahr had been speaking for years about impressionism, which runs like a red thread through all the rest of his metamorphoses. But now he has become older; expressionists, cubists, and futurists have come along, and they in turn call impressionists like Hermann Bahr dull blockheads who are only warming over the past. To Hermann Bahr's surprise the rest of the world was not greatly affected by their comments. However, he was annoyed, for he had to admit that this is exactly what he had done when he was young. He had called all the others blockheads and now they said he was one himself. And why should those who called him a blockhead be less right than he had been in saying it of others?

A bad business, you see! So there was nothing else for Hermann Bahr but to learn about expressionism, particularly as he had been asked by the people of Danzig, whom he loved so much, to speak about it. And then it was a question of finding a correct formula for expressionism. I assure you I am not making fun of Hermann Bahr. In fact, I like him very much and would like to make every possible excuse for him—I mean, that is, I like him as a cultural phenomenon.

Hermann Bahr now had to come to terms with expressionism. As you will no doubt agree, a man with a keen and active mind will surely not be satisfied to have reached the ripe age of fifty only to be called a blockhead by the next generation—especially not when he is asked to speak about expressionism to the people of Danzig who inspire him with such good thoughts. Perhaps you have seen some expressionist, cubist, or futurist paintings. Most people when they see them say, We have put up with a great deal, but this really goes too far! You have a canvas, then dashes, white ones running from the top to the bottom, red lines across them, and then perhaps something else, suggesting neither a leaf nor a house, a tree nor a bird, but rather all these together and none in particular.

But, of course, Hermann Bahr could not speak about it like this. So what did he do? It dawned upon him what expressionism is after much brooding on it. In fact, through all his metamorphoses he gradually became a brooding person. Now he realized (under the influence of the Danzig inspiration, of course!) that the impressionists take nature and quickly set it down, without any inner work on the visual impression. Expressionists do the opposite. That is true; Hermann Bahr understood that. Expressionists do not look at nature at all—I am quite serious about this. They do not look at anything in nature, they only look within. This means what is out there in nature—houses, rivers, elephants, lions—is of no interest to the expressionist, for he looks within. Bahr then went on to say that if we want to look within, such looking within must be possible for us. And what does Bahr do? He turns to Goethe, reads his works, for example, the following report:

> I had the gift that when I closed my eyes, and with bowed head imagined a flower in the center of my eye, it did not stay for even a moment in its first form, but unfolded itself and new flowers with colored as well as green leaves grew out of it. They were not natural flowers, but imaginary ones, yet regular as the roses of a sculptor.[8]

Goethe could close his eyes, think of a flower, and it would appear before him as a spiritual form and then of itself take on various forms.

> It was impossible to fix this creation welling forth in me, but it lasted as long as I wished, and neither faded nor grew stronger. I could produce the same thing by imagining an ornamental, many-colored disc, which also continually changed from the center to the periphery, exactly like the recently discovered kaleidoscope. . . .
>
> Here afterimage, memory, creative imagination, concept and idea are all at work at once, manifesting with complete freedom in the inherent living nature of the organ, without design or guidance.

Now if you are not familiar with Goethe and with the world view of modern idealism and spiritualism, you will find it impossible to make something of this right away. Therefore, Hermann Bahr continued reading the literature on the subject. He lighted on the Englishman Galton who had studied people with the kind of inner sight Goethe had according to his own description.[9] As is customary in England, Galton had collected all kinds of statistics about such people. One of his special examples was a certain clergyman who was able to call forth an image in his imagination that then changed of itself, and he could also return it to its first form through willing it. The clergyman described this beautifully. Hermann Bahr followed up these matters and gradually came to the conclusion that there was indeed such a thing as inner sight. You see, what Goethe described—Goethe indeed knew other things too—is only the very first stage of being moved in the etheric body. Hermann Bahr began to study such fundamental matters to understand expressionism, because it dawned on him that expressionism is based on this kind of elementary inner sight. And then he went further. He read the works of the old physiologist Johannes Müller, who described this inner sight so beautifully at a time when natural science had not yet begun to laugh at these things.[10]

So, Bahr gradually worked his way through Goethe, finding it very stimulating to read Goethe, to begin to understand him, and in the process to realize that there is such a thing as inner sight. On that basis he arrived at the following insight: in expressionism nature is not needed because the artist captures on canvas what he or she sees in this elementary inner vision. Later on, this will develop into something else, as I have said here before. If we do not view expressionism as a stroke of genius, but as the first beginnings of something still to mature, we will probably do these artists more justice than they do themselves in overestimating their achievements. But Hermann Bahr considers them artists of genius and indeed was led to admit with tremendous enthusiasm that we have not only external sight through our eyes, but also inner sight. His chapter on inner sight is really very fine, and he is immensely delighted to discover in Goethe's writings the words "eye of the spirit."

Just think for how many years we have already been using this expression. As I said, Bahr has even tried to master our spiritual science! From Bahr's book we know that so far he has read Eugène Lévy's description of my world view.[11] Apparently, Bahr has not yet advanced to my books, but that day may still come. In any case, you can see that here a man is working his way through the difficulties of the present time and then takes a position on what is most elementary. I have to mention this because it proves what I have so often said: it is terribly difficult for people in our age to come to anything spiritual. Just think of it: a man who has written ten novels, fourteen plays, and many books of essays, finally arrives at reading Goethe. Working his way through Goethe's writings, he comes to understand him—though rather late in his life. Bahr's book is written with wonderful freshness and bears witness to the joy he experienced in understanding Goethe. Indeed, in years past I often sat and talked with Hermann Bahr, but then it was not possible to speak with him about Goethe. At that time he naturally still considered Goethe a blockhead, one of the ancient, not-yet-impressionist sort of people.

We have to keep in mind, I think, how difficult it is for people who are educated in our time to find the way to the most elementary things leading to spiritual science. And yet, these are the very people who shape public opinion. For example, when Hermann Bahr came to Vienna, he edited a very influential weekly called *Die Zeit*. No one would believe us if we said that many people in the western world whose opinions are valued do not understand a thing about Goethe, and therefore cannot come to spiritual science on the basis of their education—of course, it is possible to come to spiritual science without education. Yet Bahr is living proof of this because he himself admits at the age of fifty how happy he is finally to understand Goethe. It is very sad to see how happy he is to have found what others were looking for all around him when he was still young. By the same token, to see this is also most instructive and significant for understanding our age. That somebody like Hermann Bahr needs expressionism to realize that one can form ideas and paint them without looking at nature shows us that the trend-setting, so-called cultural world nowadays lives in ideas that are completely removed from anything spiritual. It takes expressionism for him to understand that there is an inner seeing, an inner spiritual eye. You see, all this is closely connected with the way our writers, artists, and critics grow up and develop.

Hermann Bahr's latest novel is characteristic of this. It is called *Himmelfahrt* ("Ascension").[12] The end of the book indicates that Bahr is beginning to develop yet another burning enthusiasm on the side—all his other passions run like a red thread through the novel—namely, a new enthusiasm for Catholicism. Anyone who knows Bahr will have no doubt that there is something of him in the character of Franz, the protagonist of his latest novel. The book is not an autobiography, nor a biographical novel; yet a good deal of Hermann Bahr is to be found in this Franz. A writer—not one who writes for the newspapers; let's not talk about how journalists develop because we don't want the word "develop" to lose its original meaning—but a writer who is serious about writing, who is a true seeker, such as Hermann Bahr, cannot help but reveal his own development in the character of his protagonist. Bahr describes Franz's gradual development and his quest. Franz tries to experience everything the age has to offer, to learn everything, to look for the truth everywhere. Thus, he searches in the sciences, first studying botany under Wiessner, the famous Viennese botanist, then chemistry under Ostwald, then political economy and so on.[13] He looks into everything the age has to offer. He might also have become a student of ancient Greek under Wilamowitz, or have learned about philosophy from Eucken or Kohler.[14] After that, he studies political economy under Schmoller; it might just as well have been in somebody else's course, possibly Brentano's.[15] After that, Franz studies with Richet how to unravel the mysteries of the soul; again it might just as well have been with another teacher.[16] He then tries a different method and studies psychoanalysis under Freud.[17] However, none of this satisfies him, and so he continues his quest for the truth by going to the theosophists in London. Then he allows someone who has so far remained in the background of the story to give him esoteric exercises. But Franz soon tires of them and stops doing them. Nevertheless, he feels compelled to continue his quest.

Then Franz happens upon a medium. This psychic has performed the most remarkable manifestations of all sorts for years. And then the medium is exposed after Franz, the hero of the book, has already fallen in love with her. He goes off on a journey, leaving in a hurry as he always does. Well, he departs again all of a sudden, leaving the medium to her fate. Of course, the woman is exposed as a spy—naturally, because this novel was written only just recently.

There are many people like Franz, especially among the current critics of spiritual life. Indeed, this is how we must picture the people who pronounce their judgments before they have penetrated to even the most elementary first stages. They have not gone as far as Hermann Bahr, who after all, by studying expressionism, discovered that there is an inner seeing. Of course, Hermann Bahr's current opinions on many things will be different from those he had in the past. For example, if he had read my book *Theosophy* back then, he would have judged it to be—well, never mind, it is not necessary to put it into Bahr's words.[18] Today he would probably say there is an inner eye, an inner seeing, which is really a kind of expressionism. After all, now he has advanced as far as the inner seeing that lives today in expressionism. Well, never mind. These are the ideas Hermann Bahr arrived at inspired by the people of Danzig, and out of these ideas he then wrote this book.

I mention this merely as an example of how difficult it is nowadays for people to find their way to spiritual science. This example also shows that anyone with a clear idea of what spiritual science intends has the responsibility, as far as possible and necessary, to do everything to break down prejudices. We know the foundations of these prejudices. And we know that even the best minds of our age—those who have written countless essays and plays—even if they are sincerely seeking, reach the most elementary level only after their fiftieth year. So we have to admit that it is difficult for spiritual science to gain ground. Even though the simplest souls would readily accept spiritual science, they are held back by people who judge on the basis of motivations and reasons such as the ones I have described.

Well, much is going on in our time, and, as I have often said, materialistic thinking has now become second nature with people. People are not aware that they are thinking up fantastic nonsense when they build their lofty theories. I have often entertained you with describing how the Kant-Laplace theory is taught to children in school. They are carefully taught that the earth at one time was like a solar nebula and rotated and that the planets eventually split off from it. And what could make this clearer than the example of a drop: all you need is a little drop of oil, a bit of cardboard with a cut in the middle for the equatorial plane, and a needle to stick through it. Then you rotate the cardboard with the needle, and you'll see the "planets" splitting off just beautifully. Then the students are told that what they see there in miniature happened long ago on a much larger scale in the universe. How could you possibly refute a proof like this? Of course, there must have been a big teacher out there in the universe to do the rotating. Most people forget this. But it should not be forgotten; all factors must be taken into account. What if there was no big teacher or learned professor standing in the universe to do the rotating? This question is usually not asked because it is so obvious—too obvious. In fact, it is really a great achievement to find thinking people in what is left of idealism and spiritualism who understand the full significance of this matter. Therefore I have to refer again and again to the following fine passage about Goethe by Herman Grimm, which I am also quoting in my next book.[19]

> Long ago, in the time of his [Goethe's] youth, the famous Kant-Laplace fantasy [you see, Grimm calls it a fantasy!] about the origin and future destruction of the earth had taken root. Out of the rotating cosmic nebula our children learn about in school, a central nucleus of gas forms, which later becomes the earth. During unfathomable periods of time, this congealing globe goes through all its developmental phases, including that of

> human habitation, until it finally falls back into the sun as a piece of burnt-out slag. This long, but to the public fully comprehensible, process would need no outside intervention to run its course, except the exertion of some exterior force to keep the sun at an equal temperature. It is impossible to conceive of a more barren prospect for the future than this, urged upon us as scientifically logical and necessary. A carrion bone that a hungry dog would not go near would be a refreshing, appetizing morsel compared to this final excrement of creation our earth is supposed to be when it finally falls back into the sun. The eagerness for knowledge that makes our generation accept and believe theories of this kind is a sign of a sick imagination, a historical phenomenon it will take future scholars a lot of ingenuity to explain.

Indeed, later generations will wonder how we could ever have taken such nonsense for the truth—nonsense that is now taught as truth in all our schools! Herman Grimm goes on to say:

> Goethe never entertained such comfortless theories.... Goethe would have taken care not to derive the Darwinists' conclusions from what he had first learnt in this respect from nature and has expressed in his works.

As you know, a more spiritual understanding of Darwinism would have led to quite different results. What Grimm meant here and what I myself have to say is not directed against Darwinism as such, but rather against the materialistic interpretation of it, which Grimm characterized in one of his talks as violating all human dignity by insisting that we have evolved in a straight line from lower animals. As you know, Huxley was widely acclaimed for his answer to all kinds of objections against the evolution of human beings from the apes—I think the objections were raised by a bishop, no less.[20] People applauded Huxley's reply that he would rather have descended from an ape and have gradually worked his way up to his current world view from there, than have descended in the way the bishop claimed and then have worked his way down to the bishop's world view. Such anecdotes are often very witty, but they remind me of the story of the little boy who came home from school and explained to his father that he'd just learnt that humans are descended from apes. "What do you mean, you silly boy?" asked the father. "Yes, it's true, father, we do all come from the apes," said the boy, to which the father replied, "Perhaps that may be the case with you, but definitely not with me!" I have often called your attention to many such logical blunders perpetrated against true thinking and leading to a materialistic interpretation of Darwinism.

But these days, people always have to outdo themselves. We have not yet reached the point where people would say they have gone far enough; no, they want to go still further and outdo themselves grandiosely. For example, there is a man who is furious about the very existence of philosophy and the many philosophers in the world who created philosophies. He rails at all philosophy. Now this man recently published a volley of abuse against philosophy and wanted to find an especially pithy phrase to vent his rage. I will read you his pronouncement so you can see what is thought in our time of philosophy, by which people hope to find the truth and which has achieved a great deal, as you will see from my forthcoming book: "We have no more philosophy than animals."

In other words, he not only claims we are descended from animals, but goes on to demonstrate that even in our loftiest strivings, namely in philosophy, we have not yet advanced beyond the animals because we cannot know more than the animals know. He is very serious about this: "We have no more philosophy than animals, and only our frantic attempts to attain a philosophy and the final resignation to our ignorance distinguish us from the animals." That is to say, knowing that we know as little as cattle is the only difference between us and the animals. This man makes short work of the whole history of philosophy by trying to prove that it is nothing but a series of desperate attempts by philosophers to rise above the simple truth that we know no more of the world than the animals.

Now you will probably ask who could possibly have such a distorted view of philosophy? I think it may interest you to know who is able to come up with such an incredible view of philosophy. As a matter of fact, the person in question is a professor of philosophy at the university in Czernowitz! Many years ago he wrote a book called *The End of Philosophy* and another one called *The End of Thinking*, and he just recently wrote *The Tragicomedy of Wisdom*, where you can find the sentences I quoted. This man fulfills the duties of his office as professor of philosophy at a university by convincing his attentive audience that human beings know no more than animals! His name is Richard Wahle, and he is a full professor of philosophy at the university in Czernowitz.[21]

We have to look at things like this, for they bear witness to how "wonderfully far" we have advanced. It is important to look a bit more closely at what is necessary in life, namely, that the time has come when humanity has to resolve to take the inner Pentecost seriously, to kindle the light in the soul, and to take in the spiritual. Much will depend on whether there are at least some people in the world who understand how the Pentecost of the soul can and must be celebrated in our time.

I do not know how long it will be before my book is ready, but I have to stay here until it is finished, and so we may be able to meet again next week for another lecture.

## LECTURE TWO

June 13, 1916

# Blood and Nerves

IN SPIRITUAL science we consider all matter or substance to be a manifestation of the spiritual. But the essential question is always *how* a particular material phenomenon manifests the spiritual. The generalization that all matter is a manifestation of the spiritual really says nothing at all; at most it is an easy philosophy for lazy people. All those who seriously strive for knowledge have to study how the world's specific material phenomena manifest the spiritual.

There is a very ancient, yet ever new, saying to the effect that the human being is a microcosm. Human beings in the physical world are, in the first place, material phenomena. If we seriously believe that the human being is a microcosm, that our physical being contains the secrets of the whole cosmos, then we will think it worthwhile to examine how our physical being reveals the spiritual. If you study the physical aspect of the human being and think about it—and you'll have to think if you strive for knowledge—you will see there are two totally different kinds of substance in our physical being. It only takes ordinary thinking and observation to see that there are two fundamentally different kinds of substance in us: the blood substance, or blood material, and the nerve substance.

Of course, you may say that at first glance there are all

sorts of other substances too, muscle tissue, bone matter, and so on. But all these substances are actually built up from blood, as you will see when you study them more closely. Thus, their existence does not contradict that we have primarily two substances in us, blood substance, or blood material, and nerve substance.

One of the differences between these two substances can easily be observed; you need only consider that everything connected with the blood is involved from the inside, so to speak, in our metabolic processes. Though generated as a result of external influences, our blood is produced within us, and it in turn generates what is necessary for physical existence.

On the other hand, the most important nerves show themselves to be continuations of our sense organs. For instance, in the eyes you find the optic nerve continuing behind the eye and merging with the nerve substance of the brain. Similarly, all nerves are really continuations of our sense organs. The processes taking place in them are more or less the result of outside influences, of everything working upon us from the outside. We can say that just as magnets have two poles and just as we have positive and negative electricity, so the blood and the nerve substances are the two poles of our physical being. And these two kinds of substance are inwardly very different from each other.

If we perform an autopsy on a human being according to the methods and teachings of modern anatomy and physiology, we can put everything originating directly out of the blood next to everything built up from the outside, namely the nerve substance. Then the substances would appear to be the same. In fact, they are fundamentally different. The great and significant difference between them becomes clear if we trace the gradual development of life. We could quote a great deal from the most modern anatomy and physiology to provide further proof of this difference; however, we will not go into that right now but look at the question from the point of view of spiritual science instead.

Our blood has entered our organism as a result of processes belonging specifically to the earth. Blood is essentially of an earthly nature. You know that the development of the human being had been prepared long before the earth existed during the Saturn, Sun, and Moon phases of evolution.[1] What was prepared there did not yet have any blood. Human blood, as it flows through our veins today, was added during our earth evolution. In contrast to that, the structure and development of the nervous system contains what had long ago been prepared in the Saturn, Sun, and Moon phases of evolution through processes that preceded our earth organization.

If you investigate both the blood substance and the nerve substance in the light of spiritual science, you will readily see the tremendous difference between the two. Our nerve substance is not of the earth, but the blood substance is of the earth. Nerve substance originated in processes that took place before the formation of the earth. Our blood substance, and everything that streams and flows in it, has its origin completely in earthly processes. Our nerve substance is absolutely extraterrestrial, so to speak, and woven into us as something cosmic; it is related to the cosmos.

Our nerve substance has been transferred into the earthly realm; it exists here on the earth where we live as physical beings. Thus, we all bear something of extraterrestrial origin in us that has been transplanted onto the earth. This is a very important fact, for the nerve substance, as it rests in us, is actually dead. You need only open any current anatomy or physiology textbook to see that in terms of substance, nerve substance is the most durable in our body. It is the one most resistant to change and, like the blood substance, least subject to direct, mechanical interference from the outside. Our nerve substance is affected by influences of our sense perceptions, but it cannot be influenced directly and mechanically because it was originally a living substance and is now dead because we as earth beings carry it in us. We might say if it were not paradoxical—though it is true in a spiritual sense regardless of any paradox—that if we could take our nerve substance and raise it to a sphere beyond the influence of earth forces, it would become a marvelous, living, vibrant being.

This nerve substance is, so to speak, designed for life in the heavens, in the extraterrestrial realm, but because it is in our organism and has thus entered the earthly sphere, it dies. This is very strange, isn't it? We have this nerve substance in us that is alive in the realm of the cosmos but dead in the realm of the earth. If we were to take some of this nerve substance up beyond the reach of earthly influences, we would have a wonderful, living, luminous substance. Of course, as soon as we returned it to our earthly sphere, it would revert again to the still, lifeless condition in which it now rests within us. Our nerve substance, then, is alive in the cosmos and dead on earth.

In fact, as far as its material composition is concerned, the nerve substance we have in us is an extraterrestrial element. All this can be very clearly expressed in a symbol. As you remember, I once lectured here on anthroposophy in a more specific sense and listed the human senses. Usually people distinguish only five senses, but we counted twelve then. Human beings have twelve senses if everything that can really be called a sense is taken into account.

Ultimately, our senses are nothing but points of departure from which our nerves extend into us.

So, we really have twelve senses. And from these twelve senses nerves extend into us like little trees. This is because the nervous system that belongs to our outer senses is the expression of the passage of the sun through the twelve constellations of the zodiac, which is symbolized in the relation of our entire nervous system to each of the twelve senses. This shows that we carry in us, in the spatial relationship of our total nervous system to the twelve senses, what really exists out there in the cosmos in the sun's passage through the constellations of the zodiac.

When you look at that part of our nervous system located deeper inside us in the spinal cord, you will find the nerve fibers extending through the ring-like vertebrae of the spine. These rings in fact correspond to the months, to the orbit of the moon around the earth. Thus, the passage of each nerve fiber through the opening of the vertebrae in the spine corresponds to each day of the month—another cosmic relationship! The orbit of the moon around the earth is really symbolized in the relationship of our inner nerves to the spinal cord. Our nerve substance is entirely built up out of the heavens, out of the cosmos. We can understand this marvelous organization of the nerve substance within us only when we see in its tree-like arrangement an image of the whole starry firmament. And the forces that flow outside from star to star and express themselves in the movements of the heavenly bodies, those same forces actually flow in our nervous system, which is, however, dead in us. This connection between the organization of the cosmos and the structure of our nervous system, like many other things, reveals that the whole universe is manifest in us.

Insofar as our nervous system is built for the heavens, it is alive in the heavens, in the cosmos, but it is dead in us because it has entered the earthly sphere.

Our blood substance is quite different because it belongs entirely to the earth. Due to the inner composition of the blood, the processes taking place in it would really have to be completely earthly processes. The peculiar thing about them, however, is that they are not living processes. As you know, the mineral realm, the lifeless kingdom, developed during evolution on the earth. And the nature of our blood corresponds fully to this lifeless kingdom. Although our blood lives as long as it is in us, it is not destined for life by its inner, earthly nature. Strangely enough, our blood is alive only because it is connected to the cosmic element in us. Our nervous system is actually destined for life in the cosmos beyond the earth but is dead inside us; our blood, on the other hand, is meant to be dead in us and receives its life from outside. In a sense, the nervous system yields its life to the blood. Thus, the nervous system is dead while the blood is alive, comparatively speaking. Our blood is by its very nature dead on earth and has only a borrowed life, a cosmic life forced upon it. Life itself is not at all of our earth. That is why the nervous system must take death upon itself in order to become earthly, and why the blood has to become living to enable us as beings of earthly substance to turn to the world beyond the earth.

This is the point where all we have learned through spiritual science takes on a deeply serious character. For we have to realize that the nerve substance we have in us is by its very nature destined for life, and yet it is dead. Why is that? It is dead because it has been transplanted onto the earth. Death—as you can read in the cycle of lectures I gave in Munich—is actually the kingdom of Ahriman.[2] Thus, because our nervous system lost its life in its descent into the earthly sphere, we carry an ahrimanic element in us. And because our blood is alive—though by its very nature destined for death, that is, for mere chemical and physical processes—we have a luciferic element in us. Ahriman can exist in us because our nervous system is dead, and because our blood is alive, Lucifer can live in us. Now you can see the significant differences between these two substances; they are polar opposites, just as the North Pole is to the South Pole.

Let us now consider the realm beyond the earth, not condensing spiritual science into an abstract theory but keeping it alive so it can speak to our feelings. We look out into the universe and realize that out there is the spirit that could live in our nervous system if the latter had not descended to the earth. We can sense the spirit out there, filling the universe, the spirit belonging to our nervous system. When we then turn our thoughts to our blood, we understand that by its very nature it is actually destined only for physical and chemical processes, only for the assimilation of oxygen as it is described by anatomy and physiology. However, because it lives in us, it participates in the life of the cosmos. It has, however, a primarily luciferic life.

And now think deeply and with great sensitivity of a recurrent common theme of our talks and remember all we have said about the descent of Christ from the cosmos into our earthly sphere. Then we can link what we remember with the thoughts we have just discussed. We ourselves originated in this universe, in the cosmos. Long ago, in the Lemurian epoch, or in the course of earthly evolution in general, we descended and have connected our evolution with the earth. But by entrusting the development of our nervous system to the earth, we have consigned it to death and left its life behind in the cosmos. That life we left behind later followed us and descended in the Christ Being. In other words, the life of our nerves, which we have not been able to bear in us ever since the beginning of our earthly existence, followed us later in the Christ Being. And what did that life have to lay hold of in earthly existence? It had to lay hold of the blood! That is why we talk so much about the mystery of blood.

Our nervous system lost its cosmic life and our blood received a cosmic life, that is, life became death and death became life. They live separately in us. Yet, a new connection between them was achieved when the life of our nervous system, which had been left behind, descended to us from the cosmos, became human and entered the blood, which in turn united itself with the earth, as I have explained before.[3] And now we as human beings can reconcile the contrast between blood system and nervous system through our participation in the Christ Mystery.

The polarity we carry in us manifests in various ways. For instance, there is the material science of the outer world. It has found its culmination, its goal, in present-day natural science, which sees the world as built up out of atoms. These atoms, however, are pure fantasy; they are simply not to be found out there. Why then do we talk about atoms? Because we have in us our nervous system built up out of little globules, and we project this structure on the world outside. The world of atoms out there is nothing but a projection of our nervous system! We project ourselves into the world and thus think of it as consisting of atoms, and of our nervous system as composed of many individual ganglion-globules. Science will always tend to atomism for it originates in nerve substance. By contrast, mysticism, religion, and so forth come from the blood and do not look for atoms but always for unity. These two opposites are in conflict with each other in the world. We do not understand their conflict unless we know it is really the struggle in us between nerve substance and blood substance. There would be no conflict between science and religion if there were none in us between nerve and blood substance.

Reconciliation is found if we unite ourselves in the right way with the Christ Being that pulsates through the earth since the Mystery of Golgotha. Every feeling and experience we can have in connection with the Mystery of Golgotha contributes to this reconciliation. We have not yet advanced much in bringing about this reconciliation, but we must continue to strive for it. Even in our circles we see very often that the contrast I described manifests in one way or another. There are many among us who listen to the teachings of anthroposophy and accept them as they would accept conventional science. As a result, many people see no difference between anthroposophy and ordinary science. But we understand anthroposophy rightly only when we grasp it not just with the head, but allow every one of its utterances to kindle our enthusiasm and to live in us so that it finds its way from the nerve system to the blood system. Only when we take warmly to the truths contained in anthroposophy do we really understand it. As long as we approach it abstractly and study it as we study the multiplication tables, an arithmetic book, instruction manuals, or a cookbook, we do not understand it at all! We cannot understand anthroposophy if we study it in the same way as chemistry or botany. Only when it generates warmth in us, replenishes us with its own vibrant life, do we begin to really understand it.

Christ said: "I am with you always, even unto the end of the world." And He is with us not as one who is dead, but as a living Being among us, revealing Himself continuously. And only people so shortsighted as to fear these revelations can want us to stay with what has always held good in the past. Those who are not cowards know Christ is always revealing Himself; therefore, we may accept what He has revealed in the form of anthroposophy as a true Christ-revelation. Members have often asked me how they can establish a relationship with Christ. This is a naive question; for everything we strive for, every line we read of our anthroposophical science, is an entering into a relationship with Christ. In a certain sense, we really do nothing else. And those who seek an additional, special way of entering into a relationship with Christ are only naively expressing that they would prefer to avoid the more troublesome way of reading and studying.

My talk began like a conventional scientific talk, maybe one about anatomy or physiology, by looking at the substances in the human being, but now we find the transition to the loftiest knowledge we can have on earth: to Christology. You cannot find this transition in any other science. Spiritual science shows you that our nerve substance lost something in becoming earthly substance. But where is what our nerve substance lost? When Jesus of Nazareth was thirty years old, Christ entered his body and went through the Mystery of Golgotha. Try to warm yourselves through and through with this thought. What is lacking in our nervous system because we are living on earth, what has been replaced with an ahrimanic element, is what we find in the Mystery of Golgotha.

It is our task as human beings to take this Mystery into our blood to fill the luciferic element there with Christ, to kindle our enthusiasm so that it can live in us. Our abstract thinking is connected to the nerve substance, while our feelings, our heart and soul, enthusiasm, or mood, are connected to the blood. The relationship between nerve substance and blood substance in our organism is the same as that in our soul between abstract, cold thinking and the enthusiasm we can feel when things do not remain merely cold thoughts for us, but warm us through the spirit. This warming through the spirit does not come naturally; we have to train ourselves to attain it.

Now you can see in spiritual and physiological terms as it were, what the Mystery of Golgotha accomplished. What we had left behind in the cosmos followed us. It can now once again permeate our soul, because it did not permeate our body at the beginning of our earth existence, or we would have become automatons of the spirit. As it was, we went through a period of evolution on the earth before we were to be ensouled by what did not permeate our body right from the very beginning. This great and wonderful connection reveals the activity of the spiritual in matter.

We are not speaking here of the general, vague spiritual element woolly-headed pantheists speak of so glibly, but of the specific and definite spirit we see undergoing the Mystery of Golgotha. That is what I meant when I said that the general truism that all matter is a manifestation of the spiritual really does not say very much. We know something only when we know in detail how a specific, physical being manifests the spiritual. The findings of conventional science are an abundance of facts and material just waiting to be permeated with spiritual understanding. Spiritual understanding can penetrate them so deeply that even the most material science of all can be connected with Christology.

In our age people have difficulties finding the path connecting the nerve system with the blood system. And that is why I have shown you in several lectures how far our age is from such a spiritual understanding of the world. Last time I mentioned Hermann Bahr as an example of a man who had always been striving for the spiritual but was not able to make even the most elementary approach to the spiritual until he was already over fifty years old. I also told you that grotesque phenomena virtually dominate our cultural life, as in the case of the professor of philosophy in Czernowitz whose pronouncement I read to you.

Lest we forget his pronouncement, let me read it again: "We have no more philosophy than animals, and only our frantic attempts to attain a philosophy and the final resignation to our ignorance distinguish us from the animals." This is the quintessence of his philosophy—well, one cannot really call it philosophy; after all, according to this professor of philosophy, human beings have no more philosophy than the animals! What it amounts to is that we have reached the point where duly appointed professors of philosophy have set themselves the task of representing philosophy as ridiculous nonsense. In this case, we can see clearly how far this fellow goes. Most other philosophers do the same, only not as openly. And this truth applies not only to philosophers but also to other people who understand their task in life about as much as this philosopher does his philosophy. Therefore, they ruin every task they are appointed to fulfill as much as this philosopher ruins philosophy. However, with most of them this is not so noticeable except when they rub our noses in it as cynically as Richard Wahle does, this philosopher appointed as professor of philosophy for the destruction of philosophy.

Clearly, it is necessary—to be convinced of this necessity you need only remember my lecture a few weeks ago—to connect our striving with the era in European spiritual life when people tried to approach the spirit, although not yet with the methods of modern spiritual science. For this reason, I have given the lectures of the past winters in these difficult times and have now collected them in a book entitled *Vom Menschenrätsel* ("The Riddle of Man"), which will be published shortly.[4] This book summarizes the thinking, reflections, and contemplations of several great minds of the nineteenth century, who were striving for knowledge of the spirit though not yet with the methods of modern spiritual science. I tried to show how these great minds reached out toward the spirit even though they could not yet get there. Time will tell whether this collection of the lectures of the past winters will prove too difficult for people, even though it was written as simply as possible, and whether they will, after all, be content with merely buying it. But the important thing is to read it! Time will tell whether this book, which was written only to serve the times, will have any effect, whether it will enter into people's souls. It is a book everyone can use to prove to those outside our movement that spiritual science represents a demand of the best minds of our recent past. It did not develop arbitrarily, but is truly what the best minds have called for.

Thus, I would like to suggest that you read some of the great, spiritual works our great writers created in the nineteenth century; they are magnificent and important works. However, such good intentions often turn out strangely. As I indicated elsewhere and therefore did not repeat in this book, among the greatest of these works are the philosophical writings of Schiller, for instance, his *Letters on the Aesthetic Education of Man*.[5] Indeed, those who have read these letters with deep sympathy have done a great deal for the life of their soul. Several people have made efforts to draw the public's attention to the philosophical writings of

Schiller. One of them was Heinrich Deinhardt from Vienna.[6] In the 1860s, he wrote a splendid, extraordinarily profound little book on Schiller's world view. I don't think you can still get it in bookstores, except possibly an old, used copy in a second-hand store. It is out of print and was probably remaindered a long time ago, for nobody read what Deinhardt had to say about Schiller even though his book is one of the best things written about Schiller. Deinhardt was a teacher in Vienna whom the world has forgotten. He once had the misfortune to break his leg. Although his broken leg was set carefully, he could not get well again because he was undernourished. This man wrote one of the best books on Schiller, doubtlessly better than all the nonsense written since then, and yet he had to starve. That's the way of the world.

With my book I tried to show the relevance of great minds such as Fichte, Schelling, Hegel, Troxler, Planck, Preuss, Immanuel Hermann Fichte and a few others for our age.[7] Their works provide a completely different kind of nourishment for the soul than the writings people so often turn to in their sincere but misguided quest for the spirit. With an aching heart I have seen again and again sincerely seeking people reach for this or that book in order to find nourishment for their soul and to find a way into the spiritual world. If they had only turned to works such as Schelling's *Klara* or *Bruno*, they would have received infinite nourishment for their soul. Granted, it would have required some effort, but that would have been good for them. A certain naive searching of souls has become more and more lively and urgent in recent times. Yet, most people only reach for the soul-gunk produced by Ralph Waldo Trine or for the stuff you get when you lace some formulation or other of Buddhism, Brahminism, or something like that with a sticky sauce.[8] One can have the strangest experiences with such things. For example, I used to know a very dear man—he died recently here in Berlin— who was very enthusiastic about my writings interpreting Goethe when I first published them. Then as he grew older, he began translating a number of such soul-gunk writings, not Ralph Waldo Trine but others, from American English into German—his earlier enthusiasm evidently having been only a flash in the pan. For a long time there, people here in Europe thought they needed American-English nourishment for their souls.

Let us get a sense for what needs to be done to nourish people's souls. In the book I mentioned and also in the booklet *The Mission of Spiritual Science,* which has just been published, I tried to show what can be given even to those who are not members of our circle.[9] We can certainly hand this booklet to people who are not part of our circle. Then time will tell whether there is any understanding for the task devolving on anyone who has some idea of how necessary it is that spiritual truths stream into our present age.

I can assure you I have not merely made this or that disparaging statement in what I have said to you during these difficult times, but I have substantiated everything with details and verified it. I have not merely said philosophers are only homunculi but have quoted a particularly characteristic statement and a number of other things to give you an idea of how matters really stand and to show you that in this first third of our fifth post-Atlantean epoch everything tends to develop into homunculism, into spiritual emptiness.

People will have to penetrate more and more deeply into the difference between a merely logically correct concept and one that is true to reality. A logically correct concept is not necessarily true to reality. In my new book I have tried to elaborate what it means to think true to reality. So much that is deplorable in our cultural life comes from the belief that anything thought out logically is also necessarily true to reality. However, thinking that is true to reality is very different from merely logical and correct thinking.

For example, when you see a tree trunk lying on the ground, you see an external reality. But if you think about this tree trunk, you will find it is not a reality at all because it cannot exist as such. It necessarily has to contain the shoots that develop into branches, leaves, and blossoms. Thus, it is really a lie, this tree trunk, a "true unreality," because what it appears to be cannot exist in the nature of things. Only if you are aware that you think of something unreal when you think about a tree trunk, then your thinking is true to reality.

Thus, you see most modern sciences consist of thoughts about unrealities. Geology thinks of the earth as consisting purely of minerals. But there is no such purely mineral earth, just as the tree trunk as such does not exist. For the mineral kingdom of the earth already contains in itself plants, animals, and human beings, and only when we think of these latter kingdoms as connected with the mineral are we thinking about a reality. Geology, then, is a completely unreal science.

The outstanding feature of my new book is that I have tried to elaborate the concept of reality. Another important feature is my attempt to give at least a preliminary sketch of the imaginative thinking we will all have to develop. You will also find all kinds of comparisons and analogies in this book because I did not work with abstract, logically developed concepts. Instead, I said, for example, thinking in terms of the atomistic world view means insisting what the natural sciences think is real. It means believing when we paint a portrait, the subject of the painting can then walk around. In my book I have worked with images like this. It remains to be seen whether this unique style will be appreciated. It is the beginning of a special mode of presentation not readily found elsewhere these days.

We have to realize, however, how far people are from unbiased acceptance of these things. These days people have an incredible faith in authority. They do not look at what stands behind the authorities, but measure authority by title, rank, and official position. However, what matters is what stands behind an authority. I would like to give you a nice example to show the extent to which homunculism and thinking in mere appearances have already advanced. A man told this story as an interesting example of what homunculism in our time considers great and important—he told it with the best of intentions for he is opposed to homunculism though he is not sure what to replace it with.

There are many today who worship technology as their god, and I gave you examples of this a few weeks ago. To show the extent of this adoration of technology let me quote the following monstrosity. This is an outrageous utterance of a serious man of mature years, a doctor and a family man. He is said to be not especially outstanding or profound in any way, that is, he is considered to meet all requirements for pronouncing judgments held to be good common sense. Before the war, when the newspaper world was thoroughly amazed by the daring flight of the French aviator Pégoud, this man—a doctor and family man and in no way outstanding—this man judged the cultural value of the airplane in the style of the period, saying with great seriousness and pathos, "A screw of Pégoud's flying machine is more important than all the philosophy of Kant and Schiller, than all philosophy of all times, if you like."[10] Now, don't think this is a very unusual and rare statement. It is the sort of attitude prevailing with many people today, and it is growing stronger and stronger.

It is now more than twenty years ago, that a lady invited me to speak in her salon on Goethe after I had just given a series of public lectures. I did so, and from her circle of friends she was able to bring together quite a large audience. So I spoke to them about Goethe's *Faust* and some of his other plays.[11] The ladies took it quite well, but most of the men said that *Faust* was not a drama but science. What they meant was that in a theater one ought to see Blumenthal and not Goethe's *Faust*.[12] It is indeed true that people now are moving in a direction culminating in judgments such as the one I just read to you.

You see, today things happen quickly. Not long ago someone published the memoirs of a well-known natural scientist who died recently—at least it was something like memoirs, not really an autobiography but a book written down later by somebody else. Strictly speaking, one cannot call this memoirs. It is indeed interesting to contemplate one of the opinions expressed by this world-famous man; I don't even want to tell you his name, you would be surprised how famous he is. Indeed, he was one of the most renowned people of his day, famous and an expert in his profession, and we certainly don't want to deny his greatness. One of the things he said was, "Philosophy does not concern me at all. It is all the same to me whether the sun moves around the earth or the earth around the sun. I would only be interested in this if I were studying astronomy."[13] This man has given the world a new medical preparation; his name is on everyone's lips; yet he has never gone outside his very narrow circle and serenely admits being not particularly interested whether the earth moves around the sun or the sun around the earth. He would concern himself with that only if he were an astronomer!

I don't want to denounce or criticize anyone; this man has doubtlessly earned his fame in his own field. He liked to have his wife play the piano for him in the evening; yet he considered music merely a means to improve his concentration and was not really listening to it at all. So she played the piano for him, but he understood nothing of it and merely enjoyed his enhanced concentration. Only on Saturdays he did not want any music because then he was waiting for something still more important to him. He was fervently expecting the arrival of a detective novel, a bloodcurdling detective story in a lurid cover. He used to read such novels with special pleasure and preferred them to piano music. He loved these detective novels, the kind of trashy literature peddled on the backstairs!

Now, as I said, I am not telling you this to denounce anyone but simply to show what our times are like. We must remember that these are the authorities behind laboratory tables, behind dissecting tables. This is the spirit permeating what can indeed be very useful in the outer world and what will inevitably lead our whole culture step by step into technologization, that is, into homunculism. We must realize this danger, and, based on this insight, we have to find ways to allow the spirit to approach people. What I said here this winter was not said out of a subjective bias in favor of spiritual science, but out of insight into its inevitable significance for the present age. I believe it will be good if you will take into your souls what has been said.

We can probably meet again for another talk next Tuesday because it will surely take still another week before my book is finished.

## LECTURE THREE

June 20, 1916

# THE TWELVE HUMAN SENSES

BEFORE COMING to the topic of today's talk, I would like to say a few words about the great and grievous loss on the physical plane we have suffered in recent days. You will undoubtedly know what I mean: the day before yesterday, Herr von Moltke's soul passed through the gate of death.[1]

What this man was to his country, the outstanding part he played in the great and fateful events of our time, the significant, deep impulses growing out of human connections that formed the basis of his actions and his work—to appreciate and pay tribute to all this will be the task of others, primarily of future historians. In our age it is impossible to give an entirely comprehensive picture of everything that concerns our time. As I said, we will not speak of what others and history will have to say, but I am absolutely convinced that future historians will have very much to say about von Moltke. However, I would like to say something that is now in my soul, even if I have to express it at first symbolically; what I mean will be understood only gradually. This man and his soul stand before my soul as a symbol of the present and the immediate future, a symbol born out of the evolution of our time, in the true sense of the word a symbol of what should come to pass and must come to pass.

As we have repeatedly emphasized, we are not trying to integrate spiritual science into contemporary culture out of somebody's arbitrary impulses, but because it is needed in these times. There will not be a lasting future if the substance of this spiritual science does not flow into human development. This is the point, my dear friends, where you can see the greatness and significance we find when we think of Herr von Moltke's soul. He participated most actively in the busy life of our era, the life that developed out of the past and led to the greatest crisis humanity ever had to go through in its history. He was one of the leaders of the army and was right in the middle of the events that inaugurated our fateful present and future. Here was a soul, a personality, who did all this and, at the same time, also was one of us, seeking knowledge and truth with the most holy, fervent thirst for knowledge that ever inspired a soul in our day and age.

That is what we should think of. For the soul of this personality, who has just died, is more than anything else an outstanding historical symbol. It is profoundly symbolic that he was one of the leading figures of the outer life, which he served, and yet found the bridge to the life of the spirit we seek in spiritual science. We can only wish with all our soul that more and more people in similar positions do as he has done. This is not just a personal wish, but one born out of the need of our times. You should feel how significant an example this personality can be. It does not matter how little other people speak about the spiritual side of his life; in fact, it is best for it not to be talked about. But what von Moltke did is a reality and the effects are what is important, not whether it is discussed. Herr von Moltke's life can lead us to realize that he interpreted the meaning of the signs of the times correctly. May many follow this soul who are still distant from our spiritual science.

It is true, and we should not forget it, that this soul has given as much to what flows and pulsates through our spiritual science as we have been able to give him. Now souls are entering the spiritual world bearing within them what they have received from spiritual science. What spiritual science strives for has united with the soul of a person, who has died after a very active life. This then works as a deeply significant, powerful force in the realm we want to explore with the help of our spiritual science. And the souls now present here who understand me will never forget what I have just said about how significant it is that souls now take what has flowed for many years through our spiritual science into the spiritual world, where it will become strength and power.

I am not telling you this to assuage in a trivial way the pain we feel about our loss on the physical plane. Pain and sorrow are justified in a case like Herr von Moltke's death. But only when pain and sorrow are permeated by a sound understanding of what underlies them can they become great and momentous active forces. Take, therefore, what I have said as the expression of sorrow over the loss the German people and all humanity have experienced on the physical plane.

Let us stand up, my dear friends, and recite this verse:

Spirit of your soul, ever working Guardian!
May your wings carry
Our souls' imploring love
To the son in the spheres entrusted to your care!
United with your power,

May our prayer be a shining help
To the soul it lovingly seeks.

My dear friends, as I have often said, the occult substance that flows through our whole evolution has found its outer expression or manifestation in all kinds of more or less occult and symbolic brotherhoods and societies. In my recent talks I have characterized them in more detail as really quite superficial. We are now living in an age when the occult knowledge from the spiritual world must be given to people in a new way, as we have been trying to do for many years now, because the previous ways are obsolete. Granted, they will continue to exist for a time, but they are quite obsolete, and it is important that we understand this in the right way.

As you know, I like to call our spiritual science anthroposophy, and a few years ago when I gave lectures here, I called them lectures on anthroposophy. Last time, I referred to these lectures on anthroposophy, particularly to my emphasis on the fact that human beings actually have twelve senses. I explained that, as far as our senses are concerned, what is spread out over our nerve substance is organized according to the number twelve because the human being is in this most profound sense a microcosm and mirrors the macrocosm.

In the macrocosm the sun moves through twelve signs of the zodiac in the course of a year, and the human I lives here on the physical plane in the twelve senses. Things are certainly rather different out there in the macrocosm, especially in regard to their sequence in time. The sun moves from Aries through Taurus, and so on, and back again through Pisces to Aries as it makes its yearly course through the twelve signs of the zodiac. Everything we have in us, even everything we experience in our soul, is related to the outer world through our twelve senses. These are the senses of touch, life, movement, balance, smell, taste, sight, warmth, hearing, speech, thinking, and the sense of the I.

Our inner life moves through this circle of the twelve senses just as the sun moves through the circle of the twelve signs of the zodiac. But we can take this external analogy even further. In the course of a year, the sun has to move through all the signs of the zodiac from Aries to Libra; it moves through the upper signs during the day and through the lower ones at night. The sun's passage through these lower signs is hidden from outer light. It is the same with the life of our soul and the twelve senses. Half of the twelve are day senses, just as half of the signs of the zodiac are day signs; the others are night senses.

You see, our sense of touch pushes us into the night life of our soul, so to speak, for with the sense of touch, one of our coarser senses, we bump into the world around us. The sense of touch is barely connected with the day life of our soul, that is, with the really conscious life of the soul. You can see for yourself that this is true when you consider how easily we can store the impressions of our other senses in our memory and how difficult it is to remember the impressions of the sense of touch. Just try it and you'll see how difficult it is to remember, for example, the feel of a piece of fabric you touched a few years ago. Indeed you'll find you have little need or desire to remember it. The impression sinks down in the same way as the light fades into twilight when the sun descends into the sign of Libra at night, into the region of the night signs. And thus other senses are also completely hidden from our waking, conscious soul life.

As for the sense of life, conventional psychological studies hardly mention it at all. They usually list only five senses, the day senses or senses of waking consciousness. But that need not concern us further. The sense of life enables us to feel our life in us, but only when that life has been disturbed, when it is sick, when something causes us pain or hurts us. Then the sense of life tells us we are hurting here or there. When we are healthy, we are not aware of the life in us; it sinks into the depths, just as there is no light when the sun is in the sign of Scorpio or in any other night sign.

The same applies to the sense of movement. It allows us to perceive what is happening in us when we have set some part of our body in motion. Conventional science is only now beginning to pay attention to this sense of movement. It is only just beginning to find out that the way joints impact on one another—for example, when I bend my finger, this joint impacts on that one—tells us about the movements our body is carrying out. We walk, but we walk unconsciously. The sense underlying our ability to walk, namely, the perception of our mobility, is cast into the night of consciousness.

Let us now look at the sense of balance. We acquire this sense only gradually in life; we just don't think about it because it also remains in the night of consciousness. Infants have not yet acquired this sense, and therefore they can only crawl. It was only in the last decade that science discovered the organ for the sense of balance. I have mentioned the three canals in our ears before; they are shaped like semicircles and are vertical to each other in the three dimensions of space. If these canals are damaged, we get dizzy; we lose our balance. We have the outer ears for our sense of hearing, the eyes for the sense of sight, and for the sense of balance we have these three semicircular canals.

Their connection with the ears and the sense of hearing is a vestige of the kinship between sound and balance. The canals, located in the cavity in the petrosal bone, consist of three semicircles of tiny, very minute, bones. If they are the least bit injured, we can no longer keep our balance. We acquire our receptivity for the sense of balance in early childhood, but it remains submerged in the night of consciousness; we are not conscious of this sense.

Then comes the dawn and casts its rays into consciousness. But just think how little the other hidden senses, those of smell and taste, actually have to do with our inner life in a higher sense. We have to delve deeply into the life of our body to be able to get a sense for smell. The sense of taste already brings us a growing half-light; day begins to dawn in our consciousness. But you can still make the same experiment I mentioned before concerning the sense of touch, and you will find it very difficult to remember the perceptions of the senses of smell and of taste. Only when we enter more deeply into our unconscious with our soul does the latter consciously perceive the sense of smell. As you may know, certain composers were especially inspired when surrounded by a pleasant fragrance they had smelled previously while creating music. It is not the fragrance that rises up out of memory, but the soul processes connected with the sense of smell emerge into consciousness.

The sense of taste, however, is for most people almost in the light of consciousness, though not quite; it is still partly in the night of consciousness for most of us. After all, very few people will be satisfied with the soul impression of taste alone. Otherwise we should be just as pleased with remembering something that tasted good as we are when we eat it again. As you know, this is not the case. People want to eat again what tasted good to them and are not satisfied with just remembering it.

The sense of sight, on the other hand, is the sense where the sun of consciousness rises, and we reach full waking consciousness. The sun rises higher and higher. It rises to the sense of warmth, to the sense of hearing, and from there to the sense of speech and then reaches its zenith. The zenith of our inner life lies between the senses of hearing and speech. Then we have the sense of thinking, and the I sense, which is not the sense for perceiving our own I but that of others. After all, it is an organ of perception, a sense. Our awareness of our own I is something quite different, as I explained in my early lectures on anthroposophy. What is important here is not so much knowing about our own I, but meeting other people who reveal their I to us. Perception of the other person's I, not of our own, that is the function of the I sense.

Our soul has the same relationship to these twelve senses as the sun does to the twelve signs of the zodiac. You can see from this that the human being is in the truest sense of the word a microcosm. Modern science is completely ignorant of these things; while it does acknowledge the sense of hearing, it denies the existence of the sense of speech although we could never understand the higher meaning of spoken words with the sense of hearing alone. To understand, we need the sense of speech, the sense for the meaning of what is expressed in the words. This sense of speech must not be confused with the sense of thinking, which in turn is not identical with the ego sense.

I would like to give you an example of how people can go wrong in our time in this matter of the senses. Eduard von Hartmann, who was a most sincere seeker, begins his book

*Basic Psychology* with the following words as though he were stating a self-evident truth: "Psychological phenomena are the point of departure for psychology; indeed, for each person the starting point has to be his or her own phenomena, for these alone are given to each of us directly. After all, nobody can look into another's consciousness."[2] The opening sentence of a psychology book by one of the foremost philosophers of our time starts by denying the existence of the senses of speech, thinking, and the I. He knows nothing about them. Imagine, here we have a case where absurdity and utter nonsense must be called science just so these senses can be denied.

If we do not let this science confuse us, we can easily see its mistakes. For this psychology claims we do not see into the soul of another person but can only guess at it by interpreting what that person says. In other words, we are supposed to interpret the state of another's soul based on his or her utterances. When someone speaks kindly to you, you are supposed to interpret it! Can this be true? No, indeed it is not true!

The kind words spoken to us have a direct effect on us, just as color affects our eyes directly. The love living in the other's soul is borne into your soul on the wings of the words. This is direct perception; there can be no question here of interpretation. Through nonsense such as Hartmann's, science confines us within the limits of our own personality to keep us from realizing that living with the other people around us means living with their souls. We live with the souls of others just as we live with colors and sounds. Anyone who does not realize this knows absolutely nothing of our inner life. It is very important to understand these things. Elaborate theories are propagated nowadays, claiming that all impressions we have of other people are only symbolic and inferred from their utterances. But there is no truth in this.

Now picture the rising sun, the emergence of the light, the setting sun. This is the macrocosmic picture of our microcosmic inner life. Though it does not move in a circle, our inner life nevertheless proceeds through the twelve signs of the zodiac of the soul, that is, through the twelve senses. Every time we perceive the I of someone else, we are on the day side of our soul-sun. When we turn inward into ourselves and perceive our inner balance and our movements, we are on the night side of our inner life.

Now you will not think it so improbable when I tell you that in the time between death and rebirth the senses that have sunk deeply into our soul's night side will be of special importance for us because they will then be spiritualized. At the same time, the senses that have risen to the day side of our inner life will sink down deeper after death. Just as the sun rises, so does our soul rise, figuratively speaking, between the sense of taste and the sense of sight, and in death it sets again. When we encounter another soul between death and a new birth, we find it inwardly united with us. We perceive that soul not by looking at it from the outside and receiving the impression of its I from the outside; we perceive it by uniting with it. You can read about this in the lecture cycles, where I have described it, and also in *An Outline of Occult Science*.[3]

In the life between death and rebirth, the sense of touch becomes completely spiritual. What is now subconscious and belongs to the night side of our inner life, namely, the senses of balance and movement, will then become spiritualized and play the most important part in our life after death.

It is indeed true that we move through life as the sun

moves through the twelve signs of the zodiac. When we begin our life here, our consciousness for the senses rises, so to speak, at one pillar of the world and sets again at the other. We pass these pillars when we move in the starry heavens, as it were, from the night side to the day side. Occult and symbolic societies have always tried to indicate this by calling the pillar of birth, which we pass on the way into the life of the day side, Jakim.[4]

Our outer world during the life between death and rebirth consists of the perceptions of the sense of touch spread out over the whole universe, where we do not touch but are touched. We feel that we are touched by spiritual beings everywhere, while in physical life it is we who touch others. Between death and rebirth we live within movement and feel it the same way a blood cell or a muscle in us would feel its own movement. We perceive ourselves moving in the macrocosm, and we feel balance and feel ourselves part of the life of the whole. Here on earth our life is enclosed in our skin, but there we feel ourselves part of the life of the universe, of the cosmic life, and we feel that we give ourselves our own balance in every position. Here, gravity and the constitution of our body give us balance, and usually we are not aware of this. During life between death and a new birth, however, we feel balance all the time. We have a direct experience of the other side of our inner life.

We enter earthly life through Jakim, assured that what is there outside in the macrocosm now lives in us, that we are a microcosm, for the word Jakim means, "The divine poured out over the world is in you."

The other pillar, Boaz, is the entrance into the spiritual world through death. What is contained in the word Boaz is roughly this, "What I have hitherto sought within myself, namely strength, I shall find poured out over the whole world; in it I shall live." But we can only understand such things when we penetrate them by means of spiritual knowledge. In the symbolic brotherhoods, the pillars are referred to symbolically. In our fifth post-Atlantean epoch they will be mentioned more often to keep humanity from losing them altogether and to help later generations to understand what has been preserved in these words.

You see, everything in the world around us is a reflection of what lives in the macrocosm. As our inner life is a microcosm in the sense I have indicated, so humanity's inner life is built up out of the macrocosm. In our time, it is very important that we have the image of the two pillars I mentioned handed down to us through history. These pillars each represent life one-sidedly; for life is only to be found in the balance between the two. Jakim is not life for it is the transition from the spiritual to the body; nor is Boaz life for that is the transition from body to spirit. Balance is what is essential.

And that is what people find so difficult to understand. They always seek one side only, extremes rather than equilibrium. Therefore two pillars are erected for our times also, and we must pass between them if we understand our times rightly. We must not imagine either the one pillar or the other to be a basic force for humanity, but we must go through between the two. Indeed, we have to grasp what is there in reality and not go through life brooding without really thinking, as modern materialism does. If you seek the Jakim pillar today, you will find it. The Jakim pillar exists; you will find it in a very important man, who is no longer alive, but the pillar still exists—it exists in Tolstoyism.

Remember that Tolstoy basically wanted to turn all people away from the outer life and lead them to the inner.[5] As I said when I spoke about Tolstoy in the early days of our movement, he wanted to focus our attention exclusively on what goes on in our inner life. He did not see the spirit working in the outer world—a one-sided view characteristic of him, as I said in that early lecture. One of our friends showed Tolstoy a transcript of that lecture. He understood the first two-thirds of it, but not the last third because reincarnation and karma were mentioned there, which he did not understand. He represented a one-sided view, the absolute suppression of outer life. It is painful to see him show this one-sidedness. Just think of the tremendous contrast between Tolstoy's views, which predominate among a considerable number of Russia's intellectuals, and what is coming from there these days. It is one of the most awful contrasts you can imagine. So much for one-sidedness.

The other pillar, the Boaz pillar, also finds historical expression in our age. It too represents one-sidedness. We find it in the exclusive search for the spiritual in the outer world. Some years ago, this phenomenon appeared in America with the emergence of the polar opposite to Tolstoy, namely, Keely.[6] Keely harbored the ideal of building a motor that would not run on steam or electricity, but on the waves we create when we make sounds, when we speak. Just imagine that! A motor that runs on the waves we set in motion when we speak, or indeed with our inner life in general! Of course, this was only an ideal, and we can thank God it was only an ideal at that time, for what would this war be like if Keely's ideal had been realized? If it is ever realized, then we will see what the harmony of vibrations in external motor power really means. This, then, is the other one-sidedness, the Boaz pillar. It is between these two pillars we must pass through.

There is much, indeed very much, contained in symbols that have been preserved. Our age is called upon to understand these things, to penetrate them. Someday people will perceive the contrast between all true spirituality and what will come from the West if the Keely motor ever becomes a reality. It will be quite a different contrast from the one between Tolstoy's views and what is approaching from the East. Well, we cannot say more about this.

We need to gradually deepen our understanding of the mysteries of human evolution and to realize that what will some day become reality in various stages has been expressed symbolically or otherwise in human wisdom throughout millennia. Today we are only at the stage of mere groping toward this reality. In one of our recent talks I told you that Hermann Bahr, a man I often met with in my youth, is seeking now—at the age of fifty-three and after having written much—to understand Goethe. Groping his way through Goethe's works, he admits that he is only just beginning to really understand Goethe. At the same time, he admits that he is beginning to realize that there is such a thing as spiritual science in addition to the physical sciences. I have explained that Franz, the protagonist of Bahr's recently published novel *Himmelfahrt* ("Ascension"), represents the author's own path of development, his path through the physical sciences.[7]

Bahr studied with the botanist Wiessner in Vienna, then with Ostwald in the chemical laboratory in Leipzig, then with Schmoller at the seminar for political economy in Berlin, and then he studied psychology and psychiatry with Richet in France. Of course, he also went to Freud in Vienna—as a man following up on all the various scientific sensations of the day would naturally have to do—and then he went to the theosophists in London, and so forth. Remember, I read you the passage in question, "And so he scoured the sciences, first botany with Wiessner, then chemistry with Ostwald, then Schmoller's seminar, Richet's clinic, Freud in Vienna, then directly to the theosophists. And so in art he went to the painters, the etchers, and so on."[8]

But what faith does this Franz attain, who is really one of the urgently seeking people of the present age? Interestingly enough, he wanders and gropes, and then something dawns on him that is described as follows:

> He was no longer in a state of spiritual innocence. But wasn't there perhaps a kind of second innocence, an innocence regained? Was there not a piety of the intellect, humbled by the recognition of its own limits, wasn't there a faith for those who know, a hope born out of despair? Weren't there throughout history wise men, living in solitude and seclusion from the world, yet connected with each other through secret signs, and working wonderfully and quietly with an almost magical power in a region beyond nationalities and creeds, in the infinite, in the sphere of a purer humanity, a humanity nearer to God? Were there not even today, scattered all over the world and hidden in secret, knights of the Holy Grail? Were there not disciples of a white lodge, a lodge invisible and perhaps not to be entered but merely felt, yet working and predominating everywhere and determining human destiny? Hasn't there always been an anonymous community of holy men on earth, who do not know each other nor anything of each other and yet are working together and on one another through the very power of their prayers? Such thoughts had already much occupied him in his theosophical days, but he had obviously gotten to know

only false theosophists; maybe genuine, true theosophists did not allow themselves to be known. . . .

These thoughts occur to Franz after he has hurried through the world and has been everywhere, as I have told you, and has at last returned to his home, presumably Salzburg. That's where these thoughts occur to him, in his Salzburg home. I would like to mention in all modesty that he did not come to us; and we can get an idea of why Franz did not come to us. In his quest for people who are striving for the spirit, Franz remembers an Englishman he had once met in Rome and whom he describes as follows:

> He was a clever man in his mature years, of good family, a rich, independent bachelor, and a proper Englishman—sober, practical, unsentimental, lacking any musical or artistic sense; in short, a robust, cheerful, sensuous person. He loved fishing, rowing, sailing, eating and drinking heartily; he was a playboy disturbed in his complacency only by one single passion, the curiosity to see everything, to get to know everything, to have been everywhere—with no other ambition than to be able to say with satisfaction, regardless of what place was being talked about, that he knew this or that hotel, where Cook's had found accommodations for him, had seen the sights, and associated with notable people of rank and fame. To be able to travel more comfortably and to have access everywhere, he had been advised to become a freemason. He praised the usefulness of this association until he thought he had discovered a similar but better organized and more powerful association of a higher kind, which he now wanted to

join by all means, just as he would have made travel arrangements with another better firm than Cook's if one could have been found.

He was not to be dissuaded from his conviction that the world was governed by a small group of secret leaders, that so-called history was made by these men who were as unknown to their closest servants as those in turn were to theirs. He claimed to have followed the traces of this secret world government, of this real freemasonry of which the other was merely a most foolish copy, made by inadequate means. He thought he had found its center in Rome among the Monsignors, most of whom, of course, only played a minor role as unsuspecting pawns, whose jostling provided the cover for the four or five true leaders of the world. And, looking back, Franz still had to laugh at the funny desperation of this Englishman, who had the misfortune never to meet the real leaders but always only their pawns. However, this did not deter the man in his attempts but only served to increase his respect for this very well-guarded and impenetrable association, which he was willing to bet he would be allowed to enter some day—even if he had to stay in Rome until the end of his life and become a monk or even if he had to be circumcised.

For since he was tracking everywhere the invisible threads of a power covering the whole world like a spider web, he was not averse to hold Jews in very high esteem. And occasionally he expressed his serious suspicion that in the ultimate, innermost circle of this concealed worldwide web, Rabbis and Monsignors might be sitting together in utmost harmony, which would have been alright with him as long as they would allow him to take part in their magic.

There you have a caricature of what I have told you, namely, that there is, as it were, a kingdom within a kingdom, a small circle whose power radiates into others. But the Englishman, and Franz with him, imagined this circle to be a community of Rabbis and Monsignors; as a matter of fact, they are precisely the ones who are not in it. But you see that Franz just gropes his way here. And why? Well, he remembers once again the eccentric whims of the Englishman:

> It was only much later that it occurred to him to wonder whether perhaps someone who had not been born with such capacities could acquire them, whether one could train oneself to such powers, whether they could be learned. But the theosophical exercises soon disappointed him.

Those he had given up! You see, there is such a groping and fumbling in our time. People like Bahr reach their old age before they understand anything spiritual, and then they have such grotesque ideas as we see here. This Franz is then invited to the house of a canon. This Salzburg canon is a very mysterious personality, and of great importance in Salzburg—the town Salzburg is not named, but we can nevertheless recognize it. He is of even greater importance than the cardinal, for the whole city no longer talks about the cardinal but about *the* canon although there are a dozen canons there. And so Franz gets the idea that maybe this very man is one of the white lodge. You know how easy it is to get such ideas.

Well, Franz is invited to lunch at the canon's house. There are many guests, and the canon is really a very tolerant man; imagine, he is a Catholic canon, and yet he has invited a Jewish banker together with a Jesuit, Franz, and others, including a Franciscan monk. It is a very cheerful luncheon party. The Jesuit and the Jewish banker are soon talking—nota bene, the banker is one to whom practically everybody is indebted but who is really most unselfish in what he does and as a rule does not ask for repayment of what he apparently lends but instead only wants the pleasure of being invited to the house of a gentleman such as the canon once a year. The eager conversation between the Jesuit and this Jewish banker is altogether too much for Franz. He leaves them and goes into the library to escape their scandalous jokes, and the canon follows him.

> The library, though not big, was very select. On theology there were only the most essential works, the Bollandist writings and a good deal of Franciscan literature, Meister Eckhart, writings on the spiritual exercises, Catherine of Genoa, the mysticism of Görres and Möhler's symbolism. On philosophy there were more books: all of Kant's works, including the collected volumes of the Kant Society, also Deussen's Upanishads and his history of philosophy, Vaihinger's philosophy of the *As if*, and very many books on epistemology. Then the Greek and Latin classics, Shakespeare, Calderon, Cervantes, Dante, Macchiavelli, and Balzac in the original, but of German literature only the works of Novalis and Goethe, the latter in various editions and his scientific writings in the Weimar edition. Franz took down a volume of these and found a number of marginal notes made by the canon, who at this moment left the young monk and the Jesuit and joined Franz, saying, "Yes, no one knows the scientific writings of Goethe."

Now what the canon finds in Goethe's scientific writings is characteristic, on the one hand, of what is actually contained there and can be understood by the canon and, on the other hand, of what the canon can understand by virtue of being a Catholic canon.

> "Yes, no one knows the scientific writings of Goethe. It is a pity! In these writings, the old heathen that Goethe is supposed to have been suddenly appears in a different light, and only after reading them does one understand the end of *Faust.*"

There the canon is right. We cannot understand the end of *Faust* if we don't know Goethe's scientific views.

> "I have never been able to believe that Goethe pretended there [in *Faust*] to be a Catholic just for artistic effect. [You see, the canon in him cannot be denied, but never mind.] After all, my respect for the poet, for all poets, is too great to believe that at the moment he utters his last words, he is putting on a mask."

That is what most people believe, that Goethe really was only pretending when he wrote the magnificent, grandiose final scene of *Faust*. "But the scientific writings reveal on every page how much of a Catholic Goethe was." Yes, well, the canon calls everything he can understand, everything he likes, Catholic. We don't need to feel embarrassed about that.

> ". . . how much of a Catholic Goethe was, perhaps unknowingly and in any case without the courage of his convictions. These writings read as though the writer,

unfamiliar with Catholic truths, had unexpectedly discovered them on his own, on his own initiative, as it were. Of course, in the process some violent distortions and some oddities are inevitable, but on the whole nothing crucial, necessary, and essential is lacking, not even the dash of superstition, magic, or whatever you want to call it, that makes confirmed Protestants so suspicious of our sacred doctrine. Often I could hardly believe my own eyes. But once you are on the trail of the hidden Catholic in Goethe, you soon see him everywhere. His trust in the Holy Spirit (of course, Goethe prefers to call him 'Genius'), his deep feeling for the sacraments, which he thought were too few, his sense for penitence, his gift for reverence, and even more so the fact that in totally un-Protestant fashion he is not content with faith but always insists on the acknowledgment of God in the living deed, the pious work—this rare and most difficult realization that human beings cannot be approached by God if they do not first approach God themselves, the realization of this awesome human freedom to choose either to accept or reject the grace offered, this freedom through which alone God's grace will be deserved by those who decide to accept it—all this, even in his exaggerations and distortions, is still Catholic to the core."

For us, it would be particularly interesting to know what the canon calls "exaggerations." Well, in any case, he calls them Catholic and goes on to say:

"Therefore, as you see, I have often written in the margin the passages from the Council of Trent where the same content is expressed, sometimes even in almost the same words."

Imagine, a Catholic canon writing the resolutions of the Council of Trent next to the words of Goethe![9] In this juxtaposition you have what permeates all humanity and what we may call the core of spiritual life common to all people. This should not be taken as just so much empty rhetoric; instead it must be understood as it was meant. The canon continues:

> "And when Zacharias Werner tells us that a sentence in Goethe's *Elective Affinities* has made him a Catholic, I believe him implicitly. Of course, this is not to deny [here the canon comes through again] there is also a heathen, a Protestant, and even an almost Jewish Goethe; I don't want to claim him as an ideal Catholic."

What the canon adds to this we can be pleased to hear; well, I don't want to press my opinion on you; at least I am pleased to hear the following:

> "If Goethe had indeed been Catholic, which on the whole he was more likely to have been than the shallow and complacent run-of-the-mill monist the neo-German senior professors parade under his name. . . ."

Of course, the canon here refers to Richard M. Meyer, Albert Bielschowsky, Engel—neo-German senior professors who have written neo-German works on Goethe.[10]

You see, we are already doing what our times secretly and darkly long for, something that is indeed inevitable—this is a very serious matter.

Now please remember some of the first lectures I gave to our groups in these fateful times, where I spoke of a shattering occult experience, namely the perception that the soul of Franz Ferdinand, who was assassinated in Sarajevo, plays a special part in the spiritual world.[11] As most of you will remember, I told you his soul has attained cosmic significance, as it were. And now Bahr's novel has been published and people have been buying it for weeks. In it the Archduke Franz Ferdinand is described by a man who had hired himself out, under the guise of a simpleton, as a farmhand by a Salzburg landowner who is the brother of the protagonist Franz. Now this man disguised as a simpleton is so stubborn he has to be whipped to work. At the time of the assassination in Sarajevo, this poor fool behaves in such a way that he gets another thrashing; and imagine, when he reads the news of Franz Ferdinand's assassination in an announcement posted on the church door, this fellow says: "He had to end like this; it could not have been otherwise!"

Well, people can't help assuming he was part of the conspiracy even though the murder took place in Sarajevo while the simpleton was in Salzburg. However, such discrepancies don't trouble the people who investigate the matter: Obviously this fellow is one of the Sarajevo conspirators. And since they find books written in Spanish among his possessions, he is evidently a Spanish anarchist. Well, these Spanish books are seized and taken to the district judge, or whatever he is. He, of course, cannot read a word of Spanish but wants to get the case off his docket as quickly as possible after the poor simpleton has been arrested and brought before him. The district judge wants to push this case off on the superior court in Vienna; the people there are to figure out what to do with this Spanish anarchist. After all, the district judge does not want to make a fool of himself; he is an enthusiastic mountain climber and this is perhaps the last fine day of the season, so he wants to get things settled quickly and get going! He understands nothing of the matter. Nevertheless, he is certain of one thing: he is dealing with a Spanish anarchist.

Then he remembers that Franz had been in Spain (I told you Bahr himself was there too) and could read Spanish. Franz is to read the book and summarize it for the judge. And so Franz takes the manuscript—and what does he discover? The deepest mysticism. Absolutely nothing to do with anarchism—only profound mysticism! There is actually a great deal that is wonderful and beautiful in the manuscript. Well, according to Franz this simpleton wrote it himself because his very mysticism led him to want to die to the world. Naturally, I do not want to defend this way of proceeding. The simpleton then turns out to be in reality a Spanish infante, a crown prince, and his description fits that of the Archduke Johann who had left the imperial house of Austria to see the world. Franz could not discern the simpleton's Austrian character, but his true identity shines through the disguise, and Franz hits on the idea to say the fellow is a Spanish infante. You can imagine what this means in poor old Salzburg! The people believed they had caught an anarchist and put him into chains—now he turns out to be a Spanish infante! But this man, who knew the heir to the throne, Archduke Ferdinand, what does he say about the latter now after he himself has been unmasked as an infante and a mystic?

> The enchanted but now disenchanted prince, still in his old clothes and otherwise still the same old fellow, yet different since Franz knew the old clothes were a disguise, said with a smile, "Forgive me this deception,

which, for my feeling, wasn't really one. I have long since stopped being the infante Don Tadeo. If circumstances force me now to play his role again, the part has become much more difficult for me. To myself I was really the old simpleton, and if I ever lied at all, I lied to myself, not to you. I could not know I would inconvenience you, and I am sorry enough for that. Naturally it was all the silliest misunderstanding.

"I have known the successor to the throne well, without having actually met him; he was very dear to me, and we have been in touch albeit not in the 'local' way. [He means here in a way not on the physical plane.] He had long overstepped the limits of his earthly work and had already one foot in the realm of purely spiritual activity. He had to go over completely, I knew. In order to fulfill his work he could no longer stay here. It is only from there that his deed will be done. I only wonder why destiny hesitated so long with him. And that Sunday, as I came out of the church where in my prayers I had been assured again, when I saw the anxious crowd, I knew right away he had at last been freed. What is to happen through him, he can carry out only from the other side. Here he could only promise it; his life was only a preliminary announcement of what is to come. Only now can the deed come about. I have never been able to think of him as a constitutional monarch, with parliamentarianism and all that other humbug. He was a man of too much stature for that. But now he has seized the reins of action all at once. Only now in his death will this man live, really live. This is what I felt when I heard the news, and this is what I meant by the words I said at the time."

"It had to end like this," that's what he said at the time of the assassination. I have to admit that I was strangely and deeply moved when I read these words a few days ago in Bahr's *Himmelfahrt*. Just compare what we find in this novel with what has been said here out of the reality of the spiritual world! Try to understand from this how deeply spiritual science is rooted in reality. Try to see that those who are seeking for knowledge, albeit at first only in a groping, tentative way, are really on the same path, that they want to follow this path and that they also arrive at what we are developing here, even down to the details. After all, it is hardly likely that what I said back then could have been divulged to Hermann Bahr by one of our members. But even if that had been the case, he did at any rate not reject it, but accepted it.

We do not want to put into practice what is really only some hobby or other. We want to put into practice what is a necessity of our age and a very clear and urgent one at that. And now certain really slanderous things are making themselves felt, and we see that people nowadays are inclined to turn their sympathy to those who spread slander. It is much rarer these days for people to show sympathy for the side that is justified. Instead, precisely where injustice occurs we find people think those who have been wronged must appease and cajole the party who committed the injustice. We find this again and again. Even in our Society we find it again and again. My dear friends, today I do not feel in the mood to go into these things, and in any case that is not the point of my talk. I never mention such things except when it is necessary. But let me conclude by mentioning one more point.

In my recently published booklet, I have pointed out that what we are seeking in our spiritual science has been uniform and consistent since the beginning of our work.[12] I have also explained that it is indeed slander to talk of any kind of changing sides, of any contradictions to what we did in the early days of our movement. On page 49 you will find the following:

> In a lecture I gave in 1902 to the Giordano Bruno Society, I referred to these statements by I. H. Fichte [which seemed to me the expression of a modern intellectual movement and not merely the opinion of an individual]; that was when we made a beginning with what reveals itself now as the anthroposophical way of thinking. . ."[13]

I was referring there to a lecture held in Berlin before the German Section of the Theosophical Society was founded. Continuing along the lines of Goethe, I wanted to create in that lecture the starting point for this new movement not on the basis of Blavatsky and Besant, but based on modern spiritual life, which is independent of those two.[14] Yet there are people today who dare to say the name "anthroposophy" was only invented when, as they say, we wanted to break away from the Theosophical Society. As I explained in my book:

> This shows what we had in mind was an expansion of the modern striving for a world view to an actual observation of spiritual reality. Our aim was not to take any old views from the publications then (and even still today) called "theosophical," but to continue the striving that began with modern philosophy but then got stuck in the abstract and therefore did not gain access to the real spiritual world.

Circumstances sometimes bring about favorable situations in karma. Thus, what I wrote a few weeks ago so you can now read it no longer needs rely only on the memory of the few individuals who heard my talk to the Giordano Bruno Society back in 1902, that is, before the German Section was founded. Today I can present documentary evidence. Well, life's funny like that; due to the kindness of one of our members, Fräulein Hübbe-Schleiden, I have recently received the letters I wrote to Dr. Hübbe-Schleiden back then, just before and on the occasion of the founding of the German Section. Now, after his death, those letters were returned to me.

The German Section of the Theosophical Society was not founded until October 1902. This particular letter is dated September 16, 1902. There are a few words in this letter I would like to read to you. Forgive me, but I must begin somewhere. There was a lot of talk at that time about connecting with the theosophist Franz Hartmann, who was just then holding a kind of congress.[15] I have no intention of saying anything against Franz Hartmann today, but I have to read what I wrote in those days:

> Friedenau-Berlin, September 16, 1902. Let Hartmann continue to tell his rubbish to his people; in the meantime I want to take *our* theosophy where I will find people of sound judgment. Once we have a connection to the students [so far we have had only mediocre success with this], we will have gained much. I want to build anew, not patch up old ruins. [That is how the theosophical movement appeared to me then.] This coming winter I hope to teach a course on elementary theosophy in the Theosophical Library.[I did indeed hold this course, and one of the lectures was given dur-

ing the actual founding of the German Section. The course title is mentioned here, too.] In addition, I plan to teach elsewhere an ongoing course entitled "Anthroposophy or the Connection between Morality, Religion, and Science." I also hope to be able to present a lecture to the Bruno Society on Bruno's monism and anthroposophy. At this point, these are only plans. In my opinion, that is how we must proceed.

That was written on September 16, 1902. Here is the document, my dear friends, that can prove to you these things are not simply claims made after the fact, but they have really happened in this way. It is favorable karma that we are able to show who is right at this moment when so much slander is spread, and will increasingly be spread, about our cause.

LECTURE FOUR

June 27, 1916

# The Human Organism through the Incarnations

I WILL begin today by adding a few things to what we have said over the years about spiritual science. One of the most elementary facts we know is that human beings as they have developed through what we have called Saturn, Sun, Moon, and Earth phases of evolution are composed of four principal parts, namely physical body, etheric body, astral body, and I. We have often emphasized that merely naming the four parts of human beings and listing them is saying and doing very little. What is important is that we connect increasingly definite and concrete ideas and concepts with what arises in our soul when we speak of these four parts of the human being.

Let us first look at the physical body. We think we know it really well, or at least the physical sciences must know this body very well since they study it so much. Well, we know our physical body has to be a highly complicated creation for the simple reason that its first rudimentary form can be found as far back as the Saturn phase of evolution. That early physical form was then transformed during the Sun phase of evolution and changed further during the Moon phase of evolution, and by now it has undergone long ages of earth evolution, which have also left their imprint on our physical body. Thus, our physical body has been shaped in the course of four very long periods of time. We have to assume then a fourfold structure for this physical body.

When we ask what has come into our physical body during Earth evolution, we will only get a false idea if we rely on what ordinary life and conventional science tell us. For during earth evolution our physical body has only been remodeled, transformed, and metamorphosed. Much of it already existed, not merely in rudimentary form, but in a process of development, of unfolding, during the old Moon phase of evolution. We cannot really see much of what has been added during earth evolution if we take "see" in the true sense of the word. Actually, it is only our posture that has been changed during earth evolution; we have become upright beings, walking around with our spine perpendicular to the earth's surface. Our posture and everything connected with it has changed. Our upright physiognomy on the surface of the earth has been imprinted upon us during our evolution on earth.

When we think of a centaur, a very well-known mythological figure, we can say, based on spiritual science, that this figure of human being and horse, or generally of a human being and any animal form, is actually an imaginative representation of our physical body as it would be if we envisioned our present upright position combined with what human beings had been during the Moon phase of evolution before they became upright. Such figures or imaginations, which are preserved in mythology, conceal infinitely profound wisdom.

I wanted to mention this only as an example of the profound wisdom in such imaginations. Let us recapitulate briefly: If we really want to do justice to our physical body, we have to think of it as much more complicated than any of the physical sciences nowadays finds it convenient to do. We must realize that really only the position of the individual organs and the posture of our whole organism have been impressed upon us in the long course of earth evolution. Essentially, human development reaches very far back into the past to a time long before the earth existed.

Naturally, we must think in similar terms of the development of our higher, spiritual elements, namely, the etheric body, the astral body, and the I. Now we have to contemplate the interrelations, the interconnections, between these parts. At first glance, the physical body seems to be built out of physical substances, and as we grow, we see it constantly becoming bigger, adding on matter or inserting matter in the spaces between its limbs and its cells. Later, when we become fat—if we do—we see how more substance or matter is added on to our physical body. When we now study the etheric body in the same way, we find something similar going on. Only in this case it is not substances but movements that are added. These movements get more complicated in the course of life. In the etheric body of a newborn child we find comparatively simple and primitive movements. But gradually they become more complicated. Clearly, there is a process of multiplying, of growth and development, at work in both the physical and the etheric bodies.

Things are different in the astral body and I. In our life in the physical world, we are at first active only in our I, for it alone possesses full consciousness. When you look at a colored surface, your I is active; when you think, your I is active; when you feel, your I is active. In all your activities, even when you walk or move your hands, the I is active.

Everything you do while you are awake on the physical plane is ego activity. The ego is present in all activity.

How does ego activity express itself in relation to our other parts? How do all the things we do between waking up and falling asleep, that is, in full consciousness, manifest themselves? They manifest not in building up and growth, but in breaking down, in a depletion of the substances of the physical body and of the movements and forces of the etheric body.

For example, when you look at something red, or at anything colored, you are in a process of breakdown or depletion through the mere fact that you received an impression of the colored object. What takes place in your physical body, albeit in a very subtle sense, is a kind of killing or destruction of living substance, of living matter. To use a rather crude example, suppose you had a crystal that could still be changed and undergo transformations and imagine you exposed it to some kind of influence, for instance, the influence of light, so that the crystal would change and turn cloudy. In the same way something in your physical body becomes cloudy, and matter is being destroyed in your constitution, every time light reaches your eyes.

From the moment of waking up to the moment of falling asleep, we are destroying, albeit only in a very subtle way, our physical substance with our ego activity. Therefore, we must compensate for this by sleeping. During sleep, physical matter is restored for our use. There is a perpetual building up and breaking down going on in us. Activity when we sleep means building up of physical matter, especially its constitution; activity when we are awake, that is, ego activity, means a breaking down. Thus you have a continual, cyclical alternation: building up and breaking down, building up and breaking down. We are actually constantly being depleted, being consumed, by the activity of our I, and when we sleep, we have to regenerate ourselves.

That is why we often notice that something ascends, as it were, from our physical organism when we wake up. These are the regenerating forces, the restoring forces. When we have something pathological or diseased in our organism, even if only very slightly so, that also ascends. As long as our organism is healthy, it regenerates itself in a healthy way by the time we wake up. However, if it is sick, it works to expel the sickness upward. That is why many people and even children are in a bad mood and not cheerful when they wake up. The aftereffect of what is coming up out of the organism is still there. What spiritual science tells us about the human being and human life agrees with the phenomena of life in a wonderful way. It is only about an hour and a half after waking up that we are completely free of the forces of sickness that can rise up. This is how our I and physical body interact. This interaction plays itself out in the rhythm of sleeping and waking: building up, breaking down, building up, breaking down.

There is still another relationship that is very important although we don't notice it much in our everyday life. Our I and physical body interact in building up and depletion, and a similar relationship exists between our astral body and etheric body. The only difference is that the building up, insofar as it comes from the astral body, is completed earlier in life, and the breaking down thus begins earlier. What our astral body breaks down in our etheric body is connected essentially with the fact that we become weaker in the course of life and die when we have become totally decrepit. The relationship between our astral body and etheric body is fundamentally connected with our death. It is only because our astral body gradually consumes the forces of our etheric body, which in turn depletes, consumes, our physical body, that we can die. In a sense, then, we can observe a building up and breaking down in the interaction between our etheric and our astral body in the course of life—although this is not as rapid a succession as the alternation between sleeping and waking, it nevertheless has a certain rhythm.

We know that exerting ourselves with too much ego activity harms us. This is easy to understand because ego activity is after all a breaking-down process. If there is too much breaking down, we clearly and visibly weaken our organism. We can notice this visible weakening at first glance. But there can also be a weakening of our etheric body through the astral body since the latter can, so to speak, deplete our etheric body excessively. The most common symptom of this kind occurs when we live in a way that demands too much of our astral body, the vehicle of our passions and emotions. As you know, such a life-style can lead to permanent weakening. This impairment results from the astral body depleting the etheric body.

However, things may happen quite differently. How we gradually build up our astral body in the course of our life—beginning at birth or, let's say, at conception—is connected with our karma. Whether we have a tendency to develop strong emotions and passions in our astral body is of course connected with our karma. These passions, however, can in a way be humanly significant and meaningful. For example, let's take a quality that plays a role throughout human life and that is nevertheless a passion, albeit the noblest passion, the one that in its noblest form can develop into freedom from selfishness: love. Love is a passion, but it can become entirely free of egoism. It is the only passion that can become free of egoism. It is located in the astral body; the astral body is its vehicle.

Let us assume an artist with a true feeling for reality had been given the task to create a human form suffused and permeated through and through with the passion of love, the noble passion of love. Clearly, this artist could not be a naturalist, for naturalists have no feeling for realities but see only abstract, "naturalist" matter, so-called actuality. Every time artists had the task to create a Venus or an Aphrodite, they had to feel that the figure had to be completely suffused by this passion of love. Love has to be abundant; it has to pour itself out. What is the only thing that could happen in such a case? Obviously, not every ordinary female figure can represent Aphrodite or Venus. Consequently, then, the astral body of Aphrodite or Venus cannot be like any other female astral body, for otherwise every woman, every girl, would be an Aphrodite or a Venus—and that is not the case, is it? Thus, it is a matter of a special development of the astral body. The artist does not have to know anything about spiritual science, but he must feel as he creates a Venus that her astral body must be more developed, more strongly developed than that of a non-Aphrodite, a non-Venus.

However, as we have said, the astral body has a depleting, consuming nature. That has to be expressed in the work of art. How will the artist who really feels this, who really has a sense for the depleting astral body, set about creating a Venus? He will have to make it visible that there is something about the physical body that gradually consumes it. And here the spiritual scientist is in a different situation than a modern physician, for example.

Suppose an artist had created a Venus. As he was creating

her, he felt correctly that she had a more strongly consuming and depleting astral body than any other woman. We will see this in the slender neck and the shape of the chest. We will also see in other parts of the body that her astral body basically has a depleting nature. If the artist gives the matter physical expression, perhaps we will see in her overall shape that she will not live to a very old age. When an artist achieves such a creation, spiritual scientists will say he has a sense for the underlying reality. From this standpoint, we will say that artists, while they are creating, often feel a true spiritual reality.

However, what will a physician say, especially one who is not a spiritual scientist, when he sees such a figure created by an artist? He will say, "This is a representation of a person suffering from consumption." For indeed people who suffer from consumption also have a more strongly consuming and depleting astral body—due to their karma in an earlier incarnation—than do other people. Now, Botticelli has painted a most beautiful and wonderful Venus, which most of you will know.[1] In this picture of Venus standing on a shell, we see a physical body painted in such a way that we cannot help thinking it is based on a depleting astral body. That is why art historians disagree about this painting. Some of them admire the figure of this Venus precisely for its deviation from the so-called normal human form; they admire her slender neck and the unusual shape of her upper chest, and so forth. Others say these features are the result of Botticelli having painted a model who suffered from consumption.

Well, it is certainly possible to explain everything in a materialistic way. Probably Botticelli really did paint a consumptive model, namely, Simonetta, who died at the age of twenty-three. But that is not the point. What is important is that he knew he wanted precisely this woman to sit for his Venus, a woman who made it possible for him to paint a person whose physical body was being depleted by the astral body more quickly than is usually the case. I will pass around this reproduction of the painting although it is not good, but I don't have a better one at the moment. In this picture, you will see it is really clearly noticeable that we are dealing here with an astral body of a different constitution, namely, with an astral body depleting the physical body by means of the etheric body. You see, spiritual science can guide us and show us the way to an understanding of such things.

You will find that observation not sharpened by spiritual science is never enough to elucidate life. However, all things are illuminated when we approach them with the help of spiritual science, in everyday life as well as in art. We need to become patient and realize the human being is far more complicated than conventional science cares to acknowledge. The human being is a complicated creature, and one of the most irresponsible pronouncements frequently uttered in connection with world views is that the best explanation is always the one that is simplest. Well, it is not the simplest explanation that is the best; the best explanation is the one that correctly explains the matter. That's what we have to realize.

Now let me give you another example to show that the conventional sciences cannot get very far without using the approach of spiritual science. Remember the public lecture I gave in the *Architektenhaus* this winter where I said we have to distinguish first of all between two parts of our physical body: our head and the rest of our body. When you look at the human skeleton, you'll see the head standing out clearly, distinct from the rest of the body. In that lecture

I said that, roughly speaking, everything "hanging" from the head basically developed on earth. The condition of the human being at the end of the Moon phase of evolution, at the transition to the earth is retained only in the shape of the head. The head is a considerably older organ than the rest of our organism. The head is our oldest, most venerable part. The earth added all the rest to the head—that is, not quite all, but roughly speaking all the rest; we have to approximate these things.

When we consider that the I continues from incarnation to incarnation, we have to differentiate between the forces underlying the head and those underlying the rest of the organism. Remember, as I said, the form and shape of our head are essentially the result of our previous incarnation. How we conducted our life, how we acted in our previous incarnation, has left its mark on our organism and manifests in the following incarnation in our physiognomy, particularly in the shape of our skull.

As you may remember, I once said that the existence of reincarnation, repeated earth lives, is plainly visible in your skull, for the shape of your skull is determined by what kind of person you were in your previous incarnation. The formation of the rest of our physiognomy, our posture, whether we are fidgety or not and whether we gesture much or little—all this has a bearing on the next incarnation, when it is expressed in the shape of our face and particularly in that of the skull.

You can see how disputes about quite important things can arise. There are people who, especially according to their own opinion, are very learned in craniology. They feel a person's skull with their hands and read his or her character from it. What they say may be more or less true and can sometimes even be quite correct, but it can never be the whole truth or be exhaustive, because it is a fact that every one of us has indeed a head of his or her own. No skull is exactly like any other, for our skull is the result of our previous incarnation. The rest of our organism prepares the skull we will have in the next incarnation. Craniologists and phrenologists quarrel among themselves because they insist on generalizing where they ought to individualize. Well, every one has a head of his or her own!

It is only through intuition that we can find anything about a person's deeper nature revealed in the structure of the skull. Not only phrenologists, but science as a whole does not know what to make of the shape of the human skull. I would like to point out here that this is another area where the conventional natural sciences need to be supplemented by spiritual science.

In 1887, the famous anatomist Karl Langer gave a lecture on three truly important human heads, namely, the skulls of Schubert, Haydn, and Beethoven.[2] Karl Langer examined the anatomy of these three skulls. He emphasized that in none of them had he been able to find any indication of special musical talents, least of all in the skull of Beethoven. He underscored that from the standpoint of anatomy and physiology, Beethoven's skull was so ugly one would have expected anything else but not that the soul of Beethoven could have been active in it. Now Karl Langer is an anatomist who observed carefully in this particular case and proceeded on the basis of realities, not fantastic theories. He had to admit there is nothing to be found in these skulls that would indicate musical talents.

We know that Haydn, Schubert, and Beethoven were indeed musicians in the incarnation where the anatomist found these skulls. However, they may not have been musicians in their preceding incarnation. And we can well understand that particularly in the case of Beethoven everything that was purified in the time between death and rebirth could have come from a strong, powerful fighter. What is retained from the preceding incarnation manifests in the shape of the skull.

Langer was particularly struck by the fact that all three men had been musicians, and yet their skulls had nothing in common. There were no characteristics common to all three men precisely because they probably had completely different experiences in their previous incarnations and became musicians only in the incarnation where they had the skulls Langer examined. Their musical disposition expressed itself in their soul, while the shape of their skull was an expression of their experiences during the previous incarnation.

Eventually, arguments about these three skulls resulted. Another anatomist tried to prove Langer wrong. But the argument wasn't leading anywhere; after all, on what does a physical anatomist depend to study such matters? Of course, he will not want to hear of a previous incarnation and will therefore seize upon heredity. And Schaaffhausen, the anatomist who wanted to refute Karl Langer, observed that the shape of our skull is inherited.[3] In connection with such pronouncements, people never study what really happens in the hereditary transmission of the shape of the skull. If they did and did not proceed with the usual logic people so love to use in this area, they would soon see how unfounded it is to talk of heredity in this connection. In reality, we create the form of our skull based on the result of our previous incarnation. Granted, other elements can overlap or clash with what has come about in accordance with the preceding incarnation. We grow up in a certain environment, and especially if our feelings, our heart and soul, are attached to personalities in a particular environment, a good deal will still be impressed into the finer organization of our body. However, in essence, the skull is shaped according to the preceding incarnation.

You know, of course, how brilliantly people are trying to apply the so-called theory of genetics. There is now an erudite book, diligently researched—I really don't want to say anything against erudition in such a case; on the whole, the author really worked like a beaver to present his points. This book traces Goethe's ancestors as far back as possible. And what is the purpose of all this busy work? The objective is to show that traits that have appeared in several of a person's ancestors also emerge when the line of ancestors culminates in a genius. People think this is highly logical. However, as I have often said, it proves no more than saying if a man falls into water and is pulled out again, he will be wet.

Obviously, anyone coming from a certain line of ancestors still bears traits of this ancestry, which, after all, he or she has sought out. In order to prove that the theory of genetics really applies the way natural science assumes, one would have to start with certain traits and then show they are present in the following generations. Thus, we would have to start with the genius and then show that his or her extraordinary capacities were passed on to the offspring. But, of course, people will do nothing of the kind. After all, they could not prove that Goethe's genius was transmitted to his son or to his grandchildren, for we know all about them, don't we! Among the descendants of other people of genius this can also generally not be proved. When hereditary transmission could be proved, it was due to something quite different from physical heredity, namely to an inclination of the soul to incarnate in a particular family and to look for certain traits. Well, we have often talked about this.

You see, this is another example showing that conventional science must be complemented by spiritual science. What conventional science and everyday life have to offer us must at every turn be illuminated by the insights of spiritual science. Nowadays people have no idea how wonderfully the mysteries of cosmic evolution work on the soul when they are seen in the light of spiritual science.

I have often spoken of the fourth post-Atlantean or Greco-Latin epoch, and of our present epoch, the fifth one, and indicated how we differ from the people of the fourth post-Atlantean epoch. People of our epoch look at the art of Greek antiquity and admire the artists' keen perception, particularly in the sculptures, revealing things people in our time cannot easily perceive anymore. The crass, materialist explanation for this difference is that the ancient Greeks simply had a keener sense of sight. Besides, they could observe the human body in their games, which some people have half a mind to reinstate in this day and age. Well, those who nowadays imitate ancient Greek games certainly won't turn into Greeks, you can take my word for it; but people just love to imitate mere outer appearances.

As I have emphasized before, the ancient Greeks represented what they saw differently than we do now. This was because the Greeks still had something within them. We know the Greeks had developed their intellectual or mind soul. Our I is directed to the outside while our intellectual or mind soul is oriented to the inside and perceives our inner balance and the inner mobility of our body. The ancient Greeks lived more within themselves than we do. Consequently, the artists in ancient Greece did not work with their models as modern artists do. Instead, when the artist wanted to represent an arm, he felt within himself the shape and form of the muscle. And when he wanted to represent a movement, he felt what it is like to perform the movement himself. Yes, indeed, the ancient Greeks could do more than we because they were more within themselves.

As you know, the sentient soul developed during the Egypto-Chaldean epoch, and the intellectual or mind soul in the Greco-Latin epoch. Yet, the intellectual soul is still focused on what is inside us. It is only the I that emerges from our inner life and perceives the outer world. When the ancient Greeks watched a bird and imitated its flight with their own arms, they could feel in their arm movements how they had to sculpt the wings. In contrast, we need a model; we need to look at a real bird, and then we reproduce it in a painting or a sculpture.

It is with good reason that modern humanity has lost this faculty of inner experiencing. But we have to know and acknowledge the inner understanding of sculpture the ancient Greeks still had and we no longer have. We have to understand that when a Greek artist sculpted a person in movement, he knew out of inner knowledge, and not from looking at a model, how he had to position the legs, the toes, and the fingers.

Strictly speaking, people nowadays are unable to draw a bird in flight. In modern pictures, birds hover; they do not fly, and that is perfectly all right, but we have to understand it. We must not expect of our contemporaries what was expected of the ancient Greeks. This inner life of feeling had to be subdued so human beings could direct their I to the outside. We must not think of human evolution the way modern, materialistic Darwinists do and begin with imperfect human beings that develop into more perfect ones. Instead, we must see a parallel spiritual development that descends from the perfect state in the spiritual world down to human beings adapting themselves more and more to their physical organism. There are two streams of evolution, not just one. Thus, we can say our way of seeing things allows us to take in something that could not be perceived in earlier times. This earlier way of looking at things should not be carried over into later times, but, of course, it is occasionally carried over.

At this point, I would like to draw your attention to snapshots of people walking on the street you can find in any illustrated magazine. Snapshots reproduce the immediate outer reality; they show the person as he or she is—most of the time, that isn't very pretty. A snapshot of a bird will look very different from a painting. Now the strange thing is, when you look at a Japanese drawing of birds, you'll see it resembles a snapshot. That is a fact. There is a certain resemblance between Japanese drawings of birds in flight and a snapshot of birds. This resemblance applies even to Japanese drawings of people, because Japanese artists, more so than others, paint what a snapshot reveals—of course, we have to limit our observation to the representation of people walking.

This is because the Japanese have retained their way of seeing things from the fourth post-Atlantean epoch into the present. We, however, can no longer see things the way the Japanese do. Modern Japanese still see more correctly in the Greek sense—albeit not with the ancient Greeks' sense for beauty—than we Europeans do, for we have advanced to the fifth post-Atlantean cultural epoch. We can comprehend these things only when we consider them from the point of view of spiritual science. And when you compare Asian and European painting and sculpture, you will find the difference between the fourth post-Atlantean epoch, which has been preserved there, and our fifth post-Atlantean epoch.

You can see everywhere the necessity to bring spiritual science into things. However, in our culture today we are very far from understanding this need to bring spiritual science into outer knowledge. For the most part this is not because it is especially difficult to attain a spiritual scientific outlook; rather it is simply due to the fact that people resist it. What is described in my book *Knowledge of the Higher Worlds and Its Attainment* is relatively easy to understand.[4] People could quite easily learn this, but they resist it. Of course, I am not speaking about you, my dear friends, but our outer culture resists spiritual science. The main reason for this resistance is that our culture does not want to establish the basic prerequisites for the development of conscience in thinking, conscientiousness in thinking, or logical conscience. Here we come upon an actual sickness in the culture of our age, and spiritual scientists have to take it into account because it confronts them everywhere. This sickness is the lack of a logical conscience, of a conscience in thinking. You can make the most peculiar discoveries in this connection. We have already looked at examples of this, but let's look at one more example today.

There was a man—and he is still alive—who wanted to prove philosophically that ideals are nothing real, nothing vital. He simply wanted to make allowances for the modern view that will let ideals stand at a pinch but considers them as not really existing in the way physically perceptible things do. By the same token, this man was a philosopher and thus would have had very little to do if he did not let ideals stand. After all, the physical realm is already taken care of by the other sciences, and there must be something left for the philosopher to do.

Now, then, ideals have no intrinsic existence, but he still

wants to let them stand. Thus, he says they are just fictions, we must accept them as necessary fictions, as necessary assumptions. And this man then developed this idea into a whole philosophy, the philosophy of the *As if*; we have already talked about it earlier.[5] According to this philosophy we don't need to assume atoms exist, but we can look at the world *as if* atoms existed. We don't need to assume the soul exists, but we can look at the world *as if* it did. You see, it's a complete philosophy of the *As if*.

Now this man used an analogy to help his readers understand that we can hold on to ideals while at the same time denying them an intrinsic existence, and this analogy is typical of this philosopher's logical conscience. His analogy was of a child playing with a doll, which the child knows has no life of its own. In other words, why should we reject ideals when children do not reject dolls? Even though dolls are not alive, children treat them as though they were. Why shouldn't we do the same with ideals even though we know they have no intrinsic being?

Here we have the view that ideals have no real existence but can nevertheless be useful to us in life when we use them as little children use their dolls, which are not alive either and yet are treated like living beings. We are dealing here with a philosopher who compares ideals to dolls! Now, let us try to understand this analogy, this image. First, we have a little child playing with a doll, but this is based on the premise that the doll is at least a reproduction of a living being. The child would hardly play with the doll at all if it did not in some way resemble or represent a living being. This is the precondition. Clearly, then, we can hardly compare the doll to an ideal unless we also assume the ideal is after all a representation of something real and alive.

This philosopher's first nonsense is to use this analogy.

The second lies in saying we should base our life on ideals as if they existed. And what will come of all this? Naturally about as much as usually comes of children playing with dolls—on which he bases his recommendation—in other words, only a mere imitation of life. We are not only dealing here with a foolish analogy but also with a second error, a second foolishness. The analogy does not hold water because the comparison to a doll does not work: dolls are at least representations of living beings; ideals, on the other hand, are not supposed to represent anything. But even if they did, they would only lead to an imitation of life, not life itself.

We are dealing here with double nonsense. Here is a philosopher who perpetrates not just one but two absurdities. We could find many more such double absurdities in the sciences as well as in modern life in general. They are particularly numerous in the so-called wisdom of the world, in philosophy. When such thinking exists, when thinking has gone so far off the track, it cannot discipline itself to develop only valid analogies or at least a feeling for valid analogies—indeed, then we have no foundation for a spiritual view at all. For a spiritual view can develop only if our thinking is sound.

Therefore I would like to ask you to pay attention to what I say about the concept of reality in my new book, *Vom Menschenrätsel*.[6] We must develop a concept of reality, and not just a concept of the logical. A crystal is a self-contained reality, complete in itself. When I examine the crystal for what it is, it tells me the truth about itself. But look at a tree trunk without its roots and branches, does it also tell us the truth about itself? No, certainly not; it is telling lies as it is lying there, for it cannot exist as a tree trunk by itself. It could never exist if it did not grow in connection with roots, branches, and leaves; all these belong to the tree trunk. I find the truth about it only if I picture the tree as a whole. With the trunk by itself I have a piece cut out of the world of the senses, but this fragment is not a reality.

If our thinking is to be true to reality, we must develop a sense for what has to be included in our concepts. Only when we have a feeling that a leaf is not a reality because it cannot be thought of apart from a plant—you see, a crystal and a leaf are very different—only when we develop this sense for reality, are we ready to ascend in the right way to spiritual realities. Many things can be logical, but whether they are true to reality is another matter.

It is very easy to make mistakes in regard to this sense for reality. When I look at a painting of a figure taken out of the whole context, then I am not looking at reality, for I have to see the whole picture. If someone now objected that this painting is the result of earlier paintings by the same and other painters, and we would therefore have to look at the whole history of art, that would again be nonsense. We have to develop a sense for reality that tells us there are self-contained realities. Otherwise the only thing that would be "real" would be the whole universe.

Now that I have more or less covered the topic of today's talk and am not subtracting anything from its essence, I would like to add the following—not to say anything derogatory or disparaging, but only to throw light on the way our whole movement should be taken. We can introduce spiritual science into modern culture only if there are many people with the good will to stand by this spiritual science with the right feeling and sensitivity. I do not like to say such things, but they have to be said. You see, I try in every way possible to show that there is in our time a tendency, an impulse, toward spiritual science. That is why I quoted from Hermann Bahr's two books *Expressionismus* and *Himmelfahrt*. Here we have a man who is over fifty years old and is now beginning, after having written many plays and novels, to develop a longing for spiritual science and also for Goethe, who is so closely connected with its impulses. I tried to show that at the age of fifty Hermann Bahr had the good will to finally begin—according to his own admission—to read Goethe's works and that he slowly began to find his way—"groping" as I put it—into spiritual science and so has reached the very first elementary stages of it.

Books such as Hermann Bahr's *Expressionismus* and *Himmelfahrt* are really extraordinarily revealing because they show us that spiritual science is also—pardon the trivial expression—a matter of time. We will advance in this area only if we take things really seriously, if we have the right kind of reverence for spiritual science, and know that spiritual science is a basic impulse people seek in the current stage of our cultural development. It will always be detrimental to our cause if things are taken only superficially. It will be harmful if what we are trying to do here, and—it may be said in all modesty—what we are trying to do thoroughly, is mistaken for charlatanism, foolishness, fantasy, or other things like that. Nothing is as damaging to our cause as being mistaken for some sort of fantastic nonsense.

Now we have been working together for a long time, and gradually a seriousness toward our cause has developed as well as the ability to distinguish between it and other things that resemble it to some extent. After all, even a mongrel dog has some resemblance to a lion: they both have four legs! Ultimately, everything resembles everything else! What has to be taken into consideration above all is the seriousness of our striving, the seriousness of our work. Now, let me put it this way: in the case I'm talking about, I certainly appreciate the underlying good will and am grateful for it; yet I must discuss the symptomatic features of this case.

In my last two lectures, I explained that Hermann Bahr in a sense presented a self-portrait in the character of his protagonist Franz, who went through various experiences in life, and then came to a kind of mysticism. In other words, this is a serious book that portrays a person's whole life. Well, someone who had heard all this sent me a book, the book *Apostel Dodenscheidt* by Margarethe Böhme. It arrived with a note saying Apostel Dodenscheidt, like Hermann Bahr's Franz, had gone through all kinds of developments and had finally found his way to accepting reincarnation and karma. Well, that book by Böhme is a roman à clef of the worst kind. You only need to remember certain events that happened here in and around Berlin at one time and names such as Josua Klein and others. In this novel there is a man named Gottfried Gross, and so on. There is nothing worse than for the things I meant here to be mentioned in one breath with the events behind that roman à clef, a novel that in terms of literature and art is a very poor and inferior one to boot.

Indeed, there is a tendency to name things in the same breath whenever there is any chance to connect and confuse them. Granted, it was no sin that this has happened in this particular case—after all, the book was sent to me. Nevertheless, this shows what kinds of associations between ideas are formed and what kinds of things people will mistake for what we are seeking here out of the wellsprings of life. I do not want to reprimand but only to discuss a symptomatic occurrence. The things discussed here are not meant as those people understand them who take the absurdities in the book *Apostel Dodenscheidt* seriously. It is precisely this connecting of our cause with one or another striving that does it the most damage, and it is important that this truth stirs our souls; for those who find any resemblance here to the *Apostel Dodenscheidt* do not really understand what we are saying here.

I do not intend to deliver a philippic here, but I want to point out again that I certainly recognize and appreciate the good will in this case. Nevertheless, I have to talk about symptomatic occurrences, for what came to light here is the same thing that comes up in the world outside again and again: what is discussed and represented here is not really taken with the necessary seriousness and insight.

## LECTURE FIVE

July 4, 1916

# Balance in Life

TODAY'S TALK is connected with the broader theme we have talked about here so often recently. As we have seen, we need to look at the activities, thinking, and beliefs of our times that resist and oppose spiritual science as we understand it. We believe this spiritual science must become a necessary part of human cultural development in the present and the near future. Thus, what I have presented here is connected to the outlook of spiritual science as well as to the whole impulse or force on which our movement is based. And in this context I want to add a few remarks today.

Again and again we have to caution people against letting certain ideas and concepts that are meaningful in our spiritual science become merely empty words. We have to warn particularly against approaching the ideas of spiritual science—in many respects a new acquisition of humanity—with old ways of thinking and old habits of soul. For instance, we must not approach such conceptions as "ahrimanic" and "luciferic" with all the usual feelings and ideas these words evoke. We need only picture how the name Lucifer in southern regions brings up the concept of demons prevailing there. However, when we arrive at the spiritual scientific view of Lucifer, we should not have the same negative ideas and feelings connected with the old idea of demons. Nor should the ideas that arose in human souls when the medieval views of the devil were alive be applied unhesitatingly to our concept of the ahrimanic.

We must be aware that the world as it presents itself to us is in a state of equilibrium or balance. The beam of a scale does not come to rest in a straight horizontal position just because it is a beam, but only because equal weights hang down from it on both sides and balance each other out. It is the same with everything in our world. The world exists neither because of a state of rest nor because of nothingness, but because of the balance created by the possibility of deviating radically from what is right and good either toward Lucifer or toward Ahriman.

Anyone who says that we simply have to guard against everything ahrimanic and luciferic is in the same position as people who say they want a scale, but don't want to put weights on either side. For instance, we know there would be no art if the luciferic element did not play a role in the world. On the other hand, we also know there would be no observation and understanding of nature if the ahrimanic element did not play a part, too. It is only a matter of establishing a balance in the human heart and soul. And that is why we can fall prey to the ahrimanic and luciferic elements just when we think we are rejecting everything ahrimanic and luciferic. We can sin against reality, but we cannot suppress it!

Thus, those who want to avoid everything ahrimanic will easily fall prey to the luciferic, and those who are trying to avoid the luciferic will be easy prey for Ahriman. The point is to find the balance, to fear neither the one nor the other, and to have enough courage to face both ahrimanic fear as well as luciferic hope or desire. But our culture does not like this; on the contrary, our contemporary culture, unknowingly and without wanting to, loves the ahrimanic and the luciferic. Believing it is avoiding them, it becomes all the more completely their prey.

Talking in general terms and abstractions usually leads absolutely nowhere. We can only get somewhere if we approach these important problems in life in a concrete way. That is why I chose so many specific examples that show how one can find a balance in life, the balance between rest and movement, between unity and diversity.

Now there are philosophers, or people dealing with world views, who say they are striving for unity. That sounds very fine but is purely luciferic. Others are striving for diversity and don't want to have anything to do with unity. Though this can be fruitful today, it is ahrimanic. Only those really strive for balance who seek unity in diversity and look for diversity in such a way that it reveals unity. It is simply a matter of finding a way to really do this. I can only mention a few sins against this balance.

In our times, one such sin is perpetrated primarily in the way people view history. How do they view history? They study how events follow each other and how they are connected in time through the law of cause and effect—at least that's what people think. What happens immediately after one event is taken as its consequence, and people try to explain the latter on the basis of what preceded it. However, as a rule people's memory these days is very short, as we can see from the fact that for nearly two years now people have been talking about historical events, the events leading to this terribly tragic war, as if the world had only begun in July of 1914! They forget so easily what happened before that. From our reading we know people have forgotten what happened prior to that date. But aside from that, when people look at history at all, they link events to the ones that preceded them, and those in turn they connect with other preceding events. Thus, the individual events are strung up like beads on a necklace, and the result is then called history.

This way we will never find the truth, at least not the kind of historical truth that will help us in life. Although events do indeed follow upon one another, one of them may be far more important than another. Sometimes a particular event taking place at a particular time may mean much more for the understanding of what follows than other events happening at the same time. The point is to find the right events, the right facts. I have often called this way of looking at history a symptomatic view of history, in contrast to the merely pragmatic view so popular nowadays. The symptomatic approach to history tries to understand our inner, spiritual evolution on the basis of symptoms, and it finds at certain times particular events that are of far greater significance than other, concurrent happenings.

This approach to history is basically a Goethean one. Goethe made it part of his whole outlook not to see events simply lined up side by side. Instead, he saw events as significant for the course of human history depending on whether the spiritual revealed itself in them to a greater or lesser extent. Someday people will write the history of the current tragic conflicts by describing certain specific events of recent decades, and from these they will understand why the current situation has come about. Today is not the time to explain these facts; they would only be misunderstood. But in the future historians will report events that people now ignore when they read about them. However, if I may say so, truth shines forth from these events.

Over the last few years I have told you about all kinds of

facts with the intention to speak about the true spiritual course of events by means of them. Now, I have spoken more abstractly about the issue of history because if I had discussed certain facts in more detail—which would have clarified contemporary events—I would have had to talk about things that people don't want to hear about nowadays.

Those who do not look at history in this symptomatic way do not find the balance between the ahrimanic and the luciferic and fall prey to an ahrimanic view of history. The modern view of history is largely ahrimanic. Facts are not weighed properly. People believe they are evaluating facts and events but are not really doing it. Generally, they do not even know what the most important facts are because those are just the ones they consider the least important. But the opposite also happens, and we can talk about that in more detail. The opposite happens when people don't take facts into account at all, but develop general truths out of their hearts and souls; they carry these with them throughout life, trying to apply them everywhere. No matter how different the situations they may be in, they always try to apply the same truth. That is really a kind of luciferic exaggeration, but it is what people prefer these days. They want to have a kind of essence of truth that will never change and will carry them through each and every situation—that is what they would like. But that won't do at all. We have to find the balance.

Now I would like to explain what I mean. You see, people may go through the world, they may stand on a mountain and take in the wide expanses of nature. Well, they look at everything but don't connect it with the spiritual. Or people may go into homes where misery reigns; they look at everything, are touched by it, and feel sympathy. But what they think about the deepest mysteries of human existence is always the same; they carry the same thoughts into every situation. In the old folk wisdom, which is now on the decline, we can find a clear striving for balance in the soul. Thus it could happen that someone walked through a village at the time when there were still sundials—of course, nowadays sundials could not very easily be used for they cannot be set an hour back or ahead; that is impossible! But in the days when sundials were still of importance, someone might have passed through a village, seen a sundial, and found words written under it that were quite impressive. For example, people could find the following words under a sundial:

> I am a shadow.
> So too art thou!
> I reckon with time;
> And thou?

Just think, such profound words under a sundial, "I am a shadow. So too art thou!" A shadow cast by the sun. "I reckon with time. And thou?" Here, out of direct perception of a concrete reality, speaks the profound truth that human life is but a shadow of what works and weaves in the spiritual world. How vividly this comes to meet the weary wanderer, imprinting itself in his heart, when he steps before the sundial and sees the shadow! The sundial then points out to him: "A shadow so too art thou! I reckon with time. And thou?" Just imagine, these are profound and powerful questions for us, for our conscience: "Do you reckon with time? Are you finding your place in your time?" That is what I mean by saying balance must be sought.

It is important that people stop letting facts work side by side, each as important as the others and instead realize that there are important facts that can speak to us of great and eternal truths. Then what lives in the human soul and what is spread out in the universe can unite. We find ourselves truly united with the truth of the world only if we continuously come upon the truth in our interaction with the world, only if we don't insist on carrying *a priori* truths in us and don't walk by a sundial as we would by a plow or something like that. Instead, in looking at things, we must be instructed about the most noble and greatest striving that can light up in human souls.

This living together with outer reality, with all that is spread out throughout the universe, this feeling oneself at the right moment face to face with the eternal, is something quite different from learning out of books that this or that is an everlasting truth. No matter how often we abstractly impress upon ourselves that human life is a shadow of what happens to us in eternity, no matter how many beautiful ethical truths about the use of time we impress upon our memory, none of them will ever reach as deep as the finding of a right relationship between ourselves and outer reality. Then we will see a significance in the individual concrete fact, and only then will we find the balance in life we can never find by losing ourselves in the external world or by merely immersing ourselves deeply into our inner being. Mysticism is one-sided and luciferic; natural science is one-sided and ahrimanic. But mysticism developed through observation of external nature or observation of nature deepened to mysticism, that is balance!

Let us take another example. Suppose someone were hiking one morning in a beautiful area in the Alps, noticing the song of the birds, the beauty of the woods, perhaps even the marvelous virginal purity of the water as it babbles its way downhill in brooks, and so on. Imagine the hiker wandered for an hour, maybe, or an hour and a half, and then came upon a simple wooden crucifix. The hiker may be inwardly glad, having all the forces of gladness in his soul shaken awake because he or she has seen beautiful, great, noble, and sublime views. But the hiker is also weary and approaches this place where a simple wooden crucifix stands in the midst of beautiful and wonderfully sublime nature. On the crucifix there are the following words:

Stay your steps, wanderer,
Look on my wounds.
Wounds abide,
Hours glide.
Take heed, and guard thy way,
Beware what on the judgment day
O'er thee as verdict I shall say.

The experience we can have on reading these words can be greater and can touch our hearts more profoundly than what we may experience on seeing the figure of Christ in Michelangelo's famous painting in the Sistine Chapel. The author of the words I have just spoken is unknown. Yet, all those who understand anything about poetry know that the person who wrote the words: "Wounds abide, hours glide," is one of the greatest poets of all time. But first one has to have a feeling for this and know that true poetry is the poetry that pours out of the human soul in the right place. Not all words that rhyme, not all that passes for poetry is true poetry. But it is true poetry when out of Christianity's eternal truths there pours forth:

Stay your steps, wanderer,
Look on my wounds.

Wounds abide,
Hours glide.
Take heed, and guard thy way,
Beware what in the judgment day
O'er thee as verdict I shall say.

These are simple words, sublime words—grandest poetry! To be made aware of the greatest event in the evolution of the earth while surrounded by sublime nature and its graceful beauty means to experience with the soul the reality in the universe. This is only an example and a more profoundly touching one than the previous one of the sundial. The important thing is to develop in life so that when we meet with such things, we do not pass by reality but experience the human soul growing together with reality and maintain the balance even in our relation to what was not made by human beings, but was given by the eternal powers. We can perceive the spiritual world only when our striving is neither only one-sided mysticism, nor only one-sided observation of nature, but instead is directed toward the union of both.

I have to say this because it is part of what present-day humanity has the least real feeling for and what it can least experience. That is why spiritual science is so difficult for people to understand nowadays. What it offers is obliterated as much by a one-sided search for an all-purpose insight as by accepting the external world pretty much without seeking the symptomatic traits and the revelation of the spiritual in various events. That is what our contemporaries have the least understanding for. If they had it, there would be much less versifying and, if I may say so, much less defining. For definitions only lead people to overestimate words, and versifying leads them to misuse words. A poem such as the one under the simple crucifix—well, nobody knows who wrote it—surely originated in a time when a profound poetical sensibility lived in the hearts and souls of the people and true balance reigned in their souls.

Alas, people in our age have become inured to true poetry because there is much too much verse around, and poetry begets more poetry just as unhealthy living produces cancer. Encouraging everybody to write poems based on what already exists in poetry is the same on the cultural and spiritual level as stimulating the life process to produce cancerous growth. In this respect we have seen the most precious fruits of the art of versifying at the end of the nineteenth century. As you may know, one of the most biting critics in Berlin had to call himself Alfred Kerr, because his real name was Kempner, a name that could not be used at the end of the nineteenth century since it brought to mind Friederike Kempner.[1] Yes, she, too, was a poet. We need only remember one of her pretty poems—I won't recite many such verses, but just this one:

> America, thou land of dreams,
> Thou world of wonder, broad and long!
> Thy trees of coconut how fair,
> Thy busy solitude how strong!

This is a very striking example, but many contemporary poems, though less striking are just like this one, and many concepts formed are just like Friederike Kempner's "busy solitude." For people nowadays often have no feeling for how strongly the adjective contradicts the noun when they speak or write. These things simply must be realized; there is no other way. After all, quite a few people nowadays speak as though they did not take language to be just gesture, which is all words really are. I have pointed out to you how clumsy a theory like Fritz Mauthner's is.[2] He wants to reduce all philosophy and all world views to mere semantics and wrote three hefty volumes as well as a whole dictionary in two volumes, which lists alphabetically all philosophical terms but not a single philosophical concept.[3] He completely disregards the fact that a word relates to its concept like a gesture. People always forget this in their world view. In everyday reality it cannot be forgotten; there we cannot easily confuse a table with the word "table," and we won't expect to learn about tables from the word "table." But in philosophy and in matters of world view that is what happens all the time.

Well, Fritz Mauthner should just meet what we call in Austria a "Bohemian Privy Counselor" (*"böhmischer Hofrat"*). He would enter "Bohemian" in his dictionary and explain all sorts of things and then do the same with "Privy Counselor." However, a "Bohemian Privy Counselor" is neither a Bohemian nor a Privy Counselor; in fact, he can be a Styrian office messenger. In Austria, we call all people "Bohemian Privy Counselor" who advance in their careers on shoes that make no more noise than slippers and who push aside their rivals without the latter noticing anything. In other words, they don't have to be Bohemians or Privy Counselors. Clearly, the meaning of this expression cannot be gotten from the words alone; they are merely a gesture.

That is what we have to realize: words are gestures. The larynx makes gestures, which become audible by means of the air, just as our hands or arms make gestures, which we cannot hear only because they are too slow. The larynx makes its gestures so quickly they become audible. The only difference lies in the quickness of the larynx. And just as it is wrong to describe somebody's gesture pointing to the table rather than describing the table, so it is wrong, in the cultural and spiritual realm, to use words to get to any truths about their concepts or the things they name.

Errors of this kind occur very frequently these days. People rely completely on words. When I was a young man—well, actually not yet a young man; I was only a boy and went to school in Wiener-Neustadt in lower Austria—I learned a little verse that has kept me from setting great store by definitions and explanations of words in general. This little verse was written on a building as the motto of the house, so to speak; it reads as follows:

> I, Hans Carouser,
> Prefer wine to water.
> If I preferred water to wine,
> Carouser would be no name of mine!

That is roughly what the modern definitions of words are often like. That is, one first makes up a definition and then formulates the explanation so that it fits, for if it didn't fit, then things would not be as they are. If you remember this little verse, you will be shielded from so much that emerges these days and is clearly visible in our so-called cultural life. Much, very much appears in our age. All these things are likely to divert our attention more and more from looking at the spiritual, from realizing that spirit reigns and weaves in what is real, in everything around us.

To an ever greater extent, we, and indeed the world, are losing all connection with the spiritual. For just talking about the spiritual does not bring it to us. A gesture pointing to a reality does not have the same meaning in regard to the reality concerned as the imitation of that gesture by another person in another room does. But what will become of our world if it loses all contact with the spiritual, if it casts off all that is spiritual? It is strange that people hardly seem to notice that they are losing the connection to the spiritual world. Humanity needs world views; people do not want to live without a world view. Yet, our modern time is largely without spirituality, without faith, or even an inclination to spirituality. However, not all those who are not inclined to spirituality can make do without a world view. And then strange justifications for a world view appear!

For example, in these last few weeks, I have been thinking about a man I spent much time with around the turn of the century, between 1898 and 1901 or so. Back then he was striving for a world view but unable to construct one. He was searching for it in Haeckelism, but apparently did not find that satisfactory. Then I completely lost touch with him. Now I see that this same man, thoroughly educated in the natural sciences, is indeed still striving for a world view, but he has the most peculiar ideas about the reasons why people arrive at world views. And incidentally, he also includes religion under the category "world view." Someone who lives totally in the merely external, material understanding of facts, in the ahrimanic reality, cannot really feel justified integrating these facts into a world view. Now if he is nevertheless looking for a world view, how is he supposed to justify this search? We can see especially from this example how misguided people can be these days. Still, they are all honestly striving people.

Now this man I mentioned admits that on the basis of what the conventional sciences give us, on the basis of what is simply "the truth," one cannot build a world view. How then do we arrive at a world view? We do not get it through our senses; our intellect, which is necessarily bound to the senses, also does not lead us to a world view—so what is left?

Well, this man hit upon the idea to look for the source of a world view in a place typical for our times, namely in psycho-sexuality! How do people build their world views? Through the fact that they are sexual beings! If we were not sexual beings, we would not integrate events and facts into a world view but would merely perceive them. I would like to read you a passage typical of this man's thinking:

> If we follow Schopenhauer's thoughts to their logical conclusion, we can say that in psycho-sexuality there are supra-individual tendencies and strivings that ultimately have to be seen in connection with the metaphysical needs of human beings. These are expressed in the creation of religious feelings and ideas as well as in the formation and elaboration of integrated world views. At the same time, we find in psycho-sexuality an opposite pole, namely, a force that pulls human beings down into the depths of their darker side. Criminal instincts also spring from psycho-sexuality.

In other words, there are two poles in human nature, and both originate in psycho-sexuality. The one pole is religious feeling and thinking about a world view; the other, criminal instincts. Isn't it—I do not say sad, I say tragic—isn't it tragic to see where our time is heading?

These ideas are not to be taken lightly. Those who observe matters closely can see with what enormous speed these ideas are spreading. In my youth psychoanalysis, the Freudian theory, did not yet exist, and back then anyone who would have wanted to found it would have been considered a lunatic. Nowadays we have not only the Freudian theory, with its publications and with its representatives in all countries, but also psychoanalytical institutions all over the world where this psychoanalysis nonsense is practiced. These days, the most important and, as you have seen, even the most sacred experiences of the human soul are traced back to psycho-sexuality.

Humanity has indeed strayed very far from the paths it used to travel and to which spiritual science must lead it again. For what we are dealing with here cannot be refuted easily, because what is at stake when we speak about these things is the overall tendency of the soul, the whole form and understanding of the soul. When a pamphlet on psycho-sexuality appeared in our own Society—and a very superficially and badly written one at that—we had a big fight on our hands, which is not yet over. People could not understand why we thought such a booklet unsuitable. I told the author that the occultist is cautious in these matters because here only a very fine line, a thin spiderweb, so to speak, separates misunderstanding from the truth, and what is important is the whole attitude of the soul, and it is dangerous to speak of these things.

We will have to speak about these things for they are investigated by external science, where they will come to play a certain role. But first we must return to the direction the soul has to take so humanity can find its way to the spiritual.

In connection with the grotesque idea to look for the source of world views in psycho-sexuality, let me tell you about another fact, one sacred to all of us. I mean the fact that in the section on Paradise in the Bible, the Hebrew has been translated appropriately into our language, and we read: "And Adam knew his wife." There you have knowledge, the concept of knowledge brought into connection with sexuality. But how? It is done exactly in the opposite way! This conceals a deep mystery. Only when people will come to things that are true on this opposite path, only then will light be shed upon these things. These truths must be looked at from the point of view of the spiritual if they are not to lead us astray. In the present age we must guard against the lack of respect for spiritual research, a lack that definitely exists. In the truest sense of the word, there is a general disrespect for the spiritual world. People believe that based on their experience of what is immediately in front of them, or on yesterday's experiences, they can intervene in the course of the world to reform and improve it.

A pathetic example of this has recently caught my attention. A man allowed himself to be so affected by the present tragic events of this terrible war that he concluded it would be a disaster if peace were ever to return to the world. He concluded that the war must continue because warfare is the natural condition of humanity. He wrote:

> War is not learnt in a day. It is really fortunate that the threats of our enemies are speeding up the process of adaptation, above all this last threat of the complete destruction of our export trade. [You see, this must have been published very recently for it takes into account the Economic Conference in Paris.] Now nobody can evade the logical conclusion that peace would be a catastrophe, that war remains the only possibility. Up to now, war has been a reaction against provocation and a means to an end; from now on it will become an end in itself. From now on all those unredeemed German souls, and possibly even the most stalwart pacifists, will realize the error of their ways and see that their

> ideals are not relics but fossils. The whole nation as one man will demand eternal war. . . .
>
> Educate people to hate, to revere hatred, to love hatred, to organize hatred! Away with immature timidity, away with a false sense of shame in the face of brutality and fanaticism! Even in terms of politics Marinelli's words hold good: "More slapping, less kissing." We must not hesitate to announce blasphemously: "Ours are faith, hope, and hatred." But hatred is the greatest of these.

Yes, my dear friends, such things exist. It can never be a matter of sticking one's head in the sand like an ostrich, but only of knowing where materialism leads, especially in its latest phase, when it is denied even by its adherents. In fact, things were better in the nineteenth century, in the days of Büchner, David Friedrich Strauss, and chubby Voit, the one who analyzed the metabolism, and all the others who at least declared themselves materialists.[4] Nowadays materialism wears a hypocritical air, and people say it has long since been overcome. However, what they have put in its place, hypocritically denying it is materialism, is nothing else but materialism, an increasingly fierce materialism.

What we need, my dear friends, is Goetheanism; we need a world view that allows the soul to grow together with reality in its particular, characteristic phenomena. This Goetheanism is nothing else but the renewal of the true Christian life of feeling and experience.

Why do Orientals not understand the Mystery of Golgotha? They do not understand it because they cannot understand that one event is more significant than another. We understand the Mystery of Golgotha only when we know the difference between events, for only then can we realize that one event can give the earth its meaning. Only when we can see differences between events can we see one event as more important than another. In the Orient, we find at most a continual play of cycles, where everything is said to repeat itself. That the earth is based entirely on the fact that we have a time of preparation for the Mystery of Golgotha followed by the Mystery of Golgotha itself as the zenith of earth evolution, and then the living into it, this truth is what humanity will gradually have to understand, based on the symptomatic view of history, of course.

Everything spiritual science can give us will ultimately culminate in the Christian view of the world, which will prevail. As I have often said, spiritual science does not want to be a new kind of religion. Rather it wants to provide the tools for humanity, which would otherwise completely fall prey to materialism, to fully understand again the spiritual that is contained in Christianity. It is absolutely necessary to look with open eyes at our age, and that is much more important than any sentimental looking into it.

## LECTURE SIX

July 11, 1916

# THE FEELING FOR TRUTH

BEFORE TODAY'S talk, there will be a recitation of several poems in the first part of the evening. In these poems I have tried to express some things connected with the way we think and feel in our spiritual science. These verses were originally intended for a eurythmy performance in Dornach and were indeed first performed in eurythmy. I will soon publish them with a few words of explanation, and they will be available here in a little booklet as part of our published cycles.[1] However, before we begin, I would like to introduce the verses with a few comments.

Last time, in another context, I spoke about the art of poetry. Now we must really take seriously what I have said so often this winter, namely, that the whole impulse, the whole spirit of our spiritual science has to enter the culture of our times and bring something special to it. Poetry is after all not just a matter of expressing something one has invented or thought, but of expressing it in a certain form. Spiritual science seeks to connect the human being with the great laws of the universe, the great laws of the cosmos. The deepest impulses of spiritual science will be understood in the true sense of the word only when people realize how extensively we are actually searching for the connection between human beings and the great transcendental laws of the universe.

What is nowadays called poetry will gradually take on a new face. Granted, this is hard to understand these days, but it is true nevertheless. Though nowadays people hardly feel this way, poetry should represent what human beings experience together with the cosmos, what is drawn from the mysteries of the cosmos. All this must flow into poetic form. If we create certain mental images that are representations of what belongs to imaginative knowledge, we can then discover the laws governing the position of the twelve signs of the zodiac and the relationship of the movements of the seven planets to these twelve signs. We can also identify certain movements and laws that do not apply to all seven planets, but only to the sun and moon and their passage through the signs of the zodiac. What matters is not that we serenade what goes on in the universe, but that what speaks there in the great laws of the universe also speaks in the form of our poetry.

And today you will hear attempts at poetry where the laws that reign in the cosmos also prevail in the sequence of the lines, their relationship to each other, and in their meaning. For instance, you will hear a poem of twelve stanzas, and each stanza has seven lines. The structure of the poem is such that what the seven lines express represents the laws of the movements of the seven planets. The fact that there are exactly twelve stanzas and that the mood of the seven lines is repeated in each stanza corresponds to the laws determining the planets' orbits through the signs of the zodiac. Thus, what is going on outside in the cosmos, in the harmony of the spheres, is also in the meaning of the twelve stanzas of seven lines each. The laws of the cosmos are meant to prevail in these twelve verses of seven lines.

You will find, let us say, in the Capricorn stanza that the fourth line expresses a certain position of Mars in regard to Capricorn. The meaning of this line must be such that if you were woken up from sleep and heard only this one line from the Capricorn stanza, this Mars line, you would be able, after having developed a feeling for this, to say this line is the Mars line of the Capricorn stanza. In the same way, all the other lines have their meaning. Thus, the structure is not just superficial or merely external; it is the poem's inner structure. This is what matters.

Similarly, the short poem of quatrains is arranged so that certain movements express cosmic events. One of the poems of twelve verses is to be taken seriously; the other, as you will see, is really a satire. Now you may easily think it improper to treat "sacred things" satirically. But truly, my dear friends, if we want to advance in this sphere of a spiritual world view, one of the basic requirements is precisely that we do not forget to laugh at those things in the world that are a laughing matter when judged rightly. A lady once told a story about a man who was always in a mood of "looking up to the great cosmic revelations." He never spoke of other people at all, only of "masters," and she also said he usually made a long face.

When she told me about this man with his long, tragic face, I remembered a very interesting experience I had long ago in Vienna. Back then, there lived a man in Vienna who tried in every sort of way to live himself into spiritual spheres. He was professor of physics and mathematics at the Vienna Agricultural College, and his name was Oskar Simony, the same man who found a tragic end much later, in fact only just recently.[2] We met in Vienna—I remember it as if it had happened only yesterday—in the Salesianergasse. I knew him by sight but had never spoken to him. He did not know me at all, and we met just as two people do who pass each other on the sidewalk. I was then just a young fellow of twenty-six or twenty-seven. Oskar Simony looked at me, stopped, and began a conversation about all sorts of things spiritual—remember, I am only telling you the facts. Then he took me to his house and gave me his latest publication on the extension of the four arithmetical operations, which he had published in the old Academy of Science. All this happened just at the time when the Austrian Crown Prince Rudolf and the Archduke Johann—who, as you may know, later disappeared under the assumed name of Johann Orth—were busying themselves with the unmasking of a psychic medium and other such things.[3] Naturally, people in Vienna back then talked a great deal about these kinds of things, and Oskar Simony examined these matters scientifically. He wrote a book about tying a knot into a round ribbon of one piece, which is very interesting.[4]

Well, as we were talking, Simony paused and then said, "In dealing with these things, one needs a good sense of humor!" Indeed, that is true; for precisely when we enter into the depths of spiritual understanding, we must not forget how to laugh. In other words, we should not feel obliged to always make a long, tragic face! I am convinced that Oskar Simony lost his sense of humor in the last part of his life before he found such a tragic end.

Now there is ample opportunity to develop this sense of humor, particularly in our spiritual movement. Caricatures of the striving for the spirit love to cling to such spiritual movements. By caricatures I do not mean people, but only aspirations; the things said to sail under the colors of spiritual striving or, shall we say, of membership in a movement that has taken on spiritual striving!

That is what makes it so difficult to represent our spiritual movement in the world. Basically, there was nothing to be said—and still is nothing to be said—against some women wearing the kind of clothing I had to design for the performance of the first scene of my first mystery drama. After all, we couldn't have had modern dress on stage there. Then several women made such dresses for themselves. That is certainly praiseworthy, but then it got out of hand. I don't need to tell you about that, as it is well-known how far these things got out of hand. Then people believed such clothes absolutely called for short hair. Yes, indeed, one could hear people say that in our movement the women wore their hair short, and the men theirs quite long—which has actually happened in only a few exceptional cases. Anyway, this has led to people asking me after public lectures whether having one's hair cut short was part and parcel of being a theosophist.

Well, all this is merely a matter of appearances; however, even in matters of inner, spiritual significance people in our circle have been up to mischief many times, mischief we must strongly oppose. The things I am supposed to have said and the things that are supposedly thus and so, and on and on! Sometimes what is said seems to indicate that the person who spoke just wanted to get some attention, to put it mildly. In other words, there are excesses that make it difficult to represent our movement to people who can't help laughing when they hear about things they do not understand. They will then also laugh about what is serious and even about what is most significant. But we do not need to provoke their laughter and give them a certain justification for it with the caricatures accompanying the striving for the spiritual. These things have led me to write a satirical poem to be performed in eurythmy, which will also be presented today.

In this satire on the twelve moods of the signs of the zodiac, the planets are also used, but they are used to give you a glimpse, so to speak, of the seamy side of all this to-do about spiritual science—not of spiritual science itself, which, of course, has no seamy or dark sides at all, only its adherents do. These poems are intended to show how the intuited cosmic laws lead to true laws of form for the poetry of the future.

These verses will be recited with several by Robert Hamerling.[5] Please keep in mind that they were intended for performance in eurythmy; today they will be presented without eurythmy, but never mind.

*Program of the recitation by Frau Steiner that followed:*
*Poems by Robert Hamerling:*
*"O, let me sing in solitude," "Son and heir of eternity," "Between heaven and earth," "Nightly movement," "Spirits of Night," "Don't scold the soft tones," "Venice," "Song of life." Followed by music on the harmonium*
*"The Eagle" by Robert Hamerling*
*Poems by Rudolf Steiner:*
*"Dance of the Planets," "Pentecost," "Twelve Moods." Followed by music on the harmonium*
*"Lost Echoes" by Robert Hamerling*
*"Diamonds" by Robert Hamerling*
*"The Song of Initiation," a satire by Rudolf Steiner.*

I want to start from the same basis as in so many of our talks, namely, spiritual science as it permeates us should not live in our souls so that we simply know it in the same way we know geography, botany, or political science, and can keep it nicely separate from the rest of life. On the contrary, spiritual science should give us impulses and life forces that flow into our understanding of the reality surrounding us. This is how it must be for the sake of spiritual science and also because it has the task to intervene in our cultural life and revitalize many areas where our culture has reached a dead end. Spiritual science is to heal what is sick in our cultural and spiritual life. One thing above all must permeate the activity of our soul if we really want to enter deeply into spiritual science, and that is honesty. We will have to be so imbued with honesty that we do not waver from it in our whole understanding of life. However, we are confronted today by a view of life that is certainly not permeated by honesty in its judgments and attitudes.

Now let us take as our point of departure an event we have recently learned about. It is already a bit dishonest to think too little about such events and not to see them clearly enough in the context of life as a whole. You may have read about the shocking events that have recently taken place on a small scale, in one person's life, and must be added to those terrible, great, and gigantic blows of fate we witness in our time. Nowadays everything that is not part of the great events of the day is considered to be on a small scale.

Well, a painter, and apparently a good one at that, as the court records show, had painted pictures and signed them Böcklin, Uhde, Menzel, Spitzweg, and other famous names.[6] He had painted many such pictures and sold them to people who wanted to buy a Menzel, a Lenbach, a Böcklin. However, the painter's name was really Lehmann.[7] Lehmann was a good painter, and so his paintings were bought as genuine Böcklins, Menzels, Uhdes, and so forth. And then he was prosecuted. It was obviously a clear case of fraud. The experts held the fraud to be the greater because he was such a good painter and had been able to do so well that his paintings were indistinguishable from those painted by these famous artists. For this fraud he was sentenced to four years in prison.

Now, let me tell you a story that is the counterpart to this event. Goethe used to place a picture and its counter-picture side by side; that was his method. This is of course not so convenient as the usual way of thinking, but it throws more light on reality and truth. In Brussels, there is the Wiertz Museum, where paintings by Wiertz are exhibited.[8] One can't help but be utterly amazed at the originality of these pictures by Wiertz. They are indeed different from any other paintings; they are unique. Some of them may seem weird and crazy to strict and narrow-minded critics. Well, their opinion may not always be a valid criterion; in any case some of the paintings are very deeply moving.

Wiertz was born into a poor family at the beginning of the nineteenth century and grew up in poverty. One day, however, he was struck by the thought—and here true vocation met with extraordinary vanity; a combination that is indeed possible—that he wanted to become a painter greater even than Rubens, a successor of Rubens, a super-Rubens.[9] In post-Nietzschean times, I think we can say a super-Rubens. So he wanted to be a super-Rubens, and he certainly had talent. He got a scholarship and could go to Rome and study Italian painting. And then he painted a picture, a very large picture, a gigantic picture, of a scene from the Trojan war. It was better, indeed far better, than the average pictures you can see in exhibitions.

So, he submitted this picture to the committee of the Louvre in Paris. The committee accepted it, but hung the painting in such a way that it looked as though it had not really been accepted. You know it is a frequent practice of the committees in charge of selecting artworks for museums to hang pictures as if they did not really belong in the exhibition. But it is of course essential for a picture to be seen! When people cannot see it because it is hung in a poorly lit place, then even though the painting is on exhibit, it's as good as not really there. And since Wiertz had just as much vanity as talent, this vexed him greatly. He got very furious with Paris, went back to Brussels, and never again wrote the word "Paris" without drawing a thunderbolt above it that was striking the word. He later received other distinctions, but they did not particularly please him. For instance, he received a bronze medal from the king for something he did. However, Wiertz only said that if he could not have gold or silver, he did not need bronze either. He remained furious.

Then he wanted to test the Louvre committee again. In 1840 he sent two pictures to an exhibition. One of them he painted and signed with his name. The other he had come by in a different way. An acquaintance of his had a genuine, an admittedly genuine and significant Rubens painting. Wiertz at once scratched out the name Rubens and put in his own name instead. Thus, he sent two pictures signed Wiertz to the Louvre committee. The Louvre committee looked at them, at the two paintings by Wiertz and said, nothing doing; both are not suited for exhibition; they are both worthless daubs! But one of them was a genuine, even a quite excellent, Rubens! Thus Wiertz avenged himself; naturally he broadcast the story everywhere, and at the time it made quite a stir.

This is the counterpart to the event I told you about earlier. Think of the amount of dishonesty there is these days when people judge art. Do people buy actual works of art? No, names are what people buy. Names are bought! If somebody were to paint a picture today that was as good as any of Leonardo's—it might be a really good painting—it goes without saying people would buy Leonardo's but not the other person's painting.[10]

There have been other painters, and a newspaper wrote about them, who have taken to copying old masters because they were unable to sell their own work. When they wrote the name Leonardo or Michelangelo on their pictures, they could sell them![11] By the time it was discovered what they had done, they had already died, and so it was too late to imprison them for four years!

Such events have to be seen in the light of the dishonesty of our general culture. Lehmann would not have sold a single one of his pictures had he signed them Lehmann, but they would have been just as good as they are with another name on them. These things are very distressing. It is necessary to think about them, for they are examples of things that are becoming more and more frequent in other areas of everyday life and show how much our age needs honesty and the avowal of honesty, the striving for honesty. But striving for honesty is not within our reach if we do not have the will to face things, to deal with them, instead of quickly passing over them and ignoring them. What matters is that we concern ourselves with what is happening around us and try to understand things more deeply. If we do not make a practice of observing reality in all its depth, we cannot really get very far in understanding the impulses of spiritual science. For spiritual science is born out of true reality, and if we are to understand spiritual science, we must familiarize ourselves with the impulse of true reality.

Those who know the facts realize that people who deal with truth the way it is usually done cannot understand spiritual science. At the same time, they see that the impulses of spiritual science must enter the spiritual life of the present and the immediate future. People nowadays read everything that comes before their eyes only superficially, their books as well as life. They look only at the surface of events, skimming lightly over them. Here I would like to point out something that can be understood only when we accept to some degree the facts of spiritual science. If you look at the development of our age, you can make an astonishing discovery if you pay attention to what the human soul takes in directly and to what it takes in to preserve and work on.

Now, in our time most people who read anything read the newspapers. Newspapers don't last beyond their day, and people think the newspapers leave their soul as easily as they entered it. They imagine this compensates for the superficiality and dishonesty of our journalism, which really defy description. But things are not the way people usually believe them to be. The contents of a book does not imprint itself as deeply into the soul of most people these days, though they remember it much longer, as the contents of the short-lived newspaper. It is precisely this fleeting and transitory character of the newspaper and the fact that we do not try to remember it but want to forget it quickly—forgetting here must be quick—that allows it to imprint itself infinitely deeply into our unconscious.

I have pointed out before how quickly we must forget in the case of some newspapers. One time, we were in the area of Pirano in Istria, where the *Piccolo della Sera* is published. Now, that is an evening paper, and one day it ran a very sensational article; I don't even remember anymore what it was about. Anyway, the article took up three columns, nearly the whole of the front page. But there was still a bit of space left on that page, and there this very same article was officially disclaimed and corrected because the article was based on an error. Now this is a thing not often found: a newspaper article that is disclaimed on the very same page. Particularly the big city newspapers are ever so gradually moving in this direction.

It is important to know that what we take in so quickly and then quickly forget is actually imprinted deeply into the subconscious of our soul and works there as a force over time. It goes on working in what we can call the general spirit of the times, the ahrimanic spirit of the times. In other words, good books today have far less effect than newspaper articles. What is carefully taken in and works upon the ego, which imprints it into our memory, has much less effect than what we take in hastily from a newspaper. Please do not take this to mean that you should not read newspapers, but accept it as your karma. Obviously, I don't mean that we must avoid reading so much as a line in a newspaper. We must take newspapers as part of the karma of our age and develop the side of our being that is able to sense whether we are reading actual content, something containing true spiritual striving, or mere empty words.

Thus, one can only hope that people will once again develop a feeling for how mental and spiritual achievements come about. For this feeling is what we are so sorely lacking nowadays. We cannot distinguish between what is written well and what is written very badly. We take in the content of a well-written piece just as indifferently as we do that of a badly written piece. The difference, the capacity to distinguish, is what we have lost. How many people nowadays can tell the difference between a page written by Herman Grimm and one written by Eucken, Kohler, or Simmel, and I could name many other writers, too?[12]

Who can see that in *one* page of Herman Grimm lives the whole culture of Central and Western Europe—in his composition, in the way he forms his sentences? Who can sense that if we give ourselves over to this sentence structure, we can connect with what is ruling spiritually in the world? The usual scholarly babble, however, connects us with nothing except the eccentricities of the gentlemen, or, as we may say today, of the ladies in question. I have known scholars and spoken with them about Grimm; well, these scholars actually dared to compare Herman Grimm with Richard M. Meyer, or someone like him.[13] The initial "M" in Meyer's name was always used; Meyer never wrote his full middle name; I don't know why he was too timid to do that. Well, these scholars said Meyer's works showed clear, decisive, and strictly methodical research. Herman Grimm, on the other hand, was not to be called a real worker in the field of science; rather, he was only strolling through it. It was customary in those days to call him a stroller through the field of science because he had too few footnotes. Who nowadays can see that the whole of European culture up to the end of the nineteenth century really lives in the style of Herman Grimm's works, in his manner of presentation, regardless of the content? That is precisely what we must achieve: a sense for style, a true feeling for art even in this area, for that alone can school us in honesty. The hurried reading for content only, which aims only at getting information, is really a schooling in dishonesty, in lies.

You need only look at our modern age to see how infinitely much has to be done before people will again develop a feeling for style. Granted, we have to read newspapers nowadays, but we should also be so sensitive that the style that has gradually taken root there irritates us and drives us to distraction. This must really come about. How much this is lacking these days can be seen in countless examples, and you have no idea how little people are generally inclined to go to the bottom of things in their thinking.

I am not introducing what now follows in order to talk about national prejudices or personal likes and dislikes—after all, we must be able to understand every point of view and get a feeling for it. No, what I would like to tell you has nothing to do with all this. A few months ago, a book was published that is not available in Germany, and for good reason. It is entitled *J'Accuse, written by a German* and has been translated into all languages except German, and several hundred thousand copies have been sold throughout the world.[14] Now I am not going to speak of the accusations in this book and the very pessimistic picture it presents of the connections between Germany and the war and Austria and the war. I do not want to talk about that; everyone has his or her own point of view in these matters. The point here is not that this book presents everything in the darkest light and puts the blame exclusively on the Central European powers, while exonerating all the others, completely clearing and whitewashing them—and not just whitewashing them, but presenting them as whiter than white. That is not what I want to talk about.

What matters is that this book has evidently been distributed widely not only among people who have been corrupted by newspaper reading and read nothing else anyway, but also among people with supposedly enlightened minds. Now this book is trashy literature of the very worst kind imaginable, quite apart from its point of view. If you just read it as it is, you will find in terms of form, in terms of sentence structure, a piece of trashy literature, really artistically abominable literature. It is the artistic side I want to look at here, regardless of the point of view; for I can perfectly well understand a point of view opposed to mine, or indeed any point of view. But what is so infinitely sad in this case is that people did not feel that anyone who writes so abominably badly—in his sentence structure, his thinking, and logic—comes into consideration only for those readers who do not go in for respectable literature but only for stuff that's peddled on the backstairs.

I would not be speaking about this today if the subject had not been revived the day before yesterday in an article in the *Vossische Zeitung*, which used to be a gossipy rag but is now a modern newspaper. The article was written by Dr. F. Oppenheimer, an untenured extramural lecturer, and deals with this book as well as with a very successful reply published as *Anti-J'accuse*. [15] However, Dr. Oppenheimer starts out in a strange way by explaining that this book *J'Accuse* had been brought to his attention by a man from one of the neutral countries whom he had always considered one of the most outstanding and most unappreciated authors of our time. Then Oppenheimer goes on to talk about his own impressions of the book. He has at least some idea of how badly the book is written—and that is what I want to emphasize here—but I was anxious to see whether he would draw any conclusions from this insight. It seemed to me that Oppenheimer's thoughts and feelings about the book should have led him to question whether he had been in full possession of his faculties when he believed the man great who recommended such an abominable book as something special. But he did not come to that conclusion in this article.

Now I am not saying this to criticize this particular case, but to point out that it is a typical one. People just skim over the facts these days. After all, isn't this case suited to make Oppenheimer ask himself what his judgment is worth when he had taken a man for important who later tried to foist such a book off on him as significant? Is this not something that leads necessarily to some self-knowledge? Clearly, drawing the obvious conclusions from the situations confronting us now in such a terrible way is not a priority in the souls of many people. We can see the basic character and structure of contemporary spiritual life in just such typical examples. We must really feel that the basic shortcomings of our time are expressed in such things, and we must not ignore them as if they were of no importance.

These things are tremendously important, for they show on a small scale what I pointed to on a larger scale when I said that nowadays many people believe themselves to be good Christians though they have not even managed to be good Turks! Remember, I once read you a short passage from the Koran to show that Turks who know their Koran believe much more about Jesus than many modern pastors do. It is the same all over again but now on a field where the mighty facts of existence arise before the soul. The same mistake, however, the same type of mistake, meets us everywhere in our daily life, in the terrible superficiality of modern everyday life, which is really nothing else but dishonesty. We must go beyond that if all talking about spiritual science is not to be a washout for our time. The important thing is that spiritual science be more than just a failure and a waste.

We have to realize that in the nineteenth century and so far also in the twentieth century we have been wedged into a spiritual scientific development that has influenced modern thinking and feeling from two sides. There have been two streams, left and right, so to speak, and we have been wedged in between them. And now we have to extricate ourselves. Just this winter I have devoted a good many of my talks to drawing your attention to the fundamentals leading to what is thought nowadays. Truly, it is possible to show in many different symptoms what prevails these days. I have showed you this by drawing your attention to many occult movements active in different societies. I have told you that to a large extent the direction and attitude of modern thinking go back to the beginning of the fifth post-Atlantean epoch, when the predominating spirit lived in the accomplishments of Bacon, Shakespeare, and Jacob Böhme.[16] This had to be so. However, we are now at a point where we have to overcome what was rightfully inaugurated at the beginning of the fifth post-Atlantean epoch.

This is what I wanted to present in my new book *Vom Menschenrätsel*.[17] I wanted to explain the spiritual streams to which the fifth post-Atlantean epoch led, especially in Central Europe, and that the way out through spiritual science must be found. Time will tell whether this book, into which I really put all my heart—sometimes spending two whole days on a sentence that takes up a quarter of a page in order to be able to justify every word and turn of phrase—whether it will be read properly or just as badly as previous books.

You see, my dear friends, all our reflections amount to the insight that we must find in our soul the elements, the forces, to take in the Mystery of Golgotha in a new way. However, only those can understand the Mystery of Golgotha who do not seek this understanding with the forces of the physical body but by means independent of the physical body. Now, you may object that then the Mystery of Golgotha, the true wellspring of life for Christianity, can be understood only by people who have gone through esoteric development. Well, this is not the case, definitely not. Up to now people have indeed been able, even without spiritual science, to experience this freedom of the soul from the body necessary to understand the Mystery of Golgotha. But the number of those who understood dwindled while the number of those who opposed this true understanding grew ever larger.

Just think of one of the symptoms of this development: in earlier centuries, people were also reading the four Gospels and found the force contained in them. Thus, they approached an emotional and psychological understanding of the Mystery of Golgotha. Then came the people of the nineteenth century who were naturally more clever than their ancestors and discovered that the four Gospels contradict each other! How could their intellect avoid seeing that the Gospels contradicted each other? Great pains were taken to find all the contradictions and to unearth a core common to all Gospels. Not much came of all this, but the attempt made many people famous in the course of the nineteenth and even in the twentieth century. Well, are people of earlier centuries supposed to not have seen that the Gospels contradict each other? Were they really so foolish that they didn't see that the Gospel of Matthew differs from the Gospel of John? Or, perhaps, has it just not occurred to nineteenth century people that their ancestors had a different sort of understanding, sought understanding with a quite different organ of their soul? You can answer that question for yourselves on the basis of what you have learned of spiritual science.

However, the days are gone when people could understand Christianity and the Mystery of Golgotha without taking the path of spiritual science. The number of people who can understand Christianity without spiritual science will become smaller and smaller. Spiritual science will become more and more an indispensable path to the understanding of the Mystery of Golgotha, which has to be understood with the etheric body. Everything else can be understood with the physical body. But spiritual science alone can prepare us for an understanding of all that has to be understood with the etheric body. Therefore either spiritual science will be fortunate and succeed, or there will be no further spread of Christianity because the Mystery of Golgotha will not be understood. In this respect we are still misunderstood by all those who think they are on the right path.

I have to tell the following story again and again. A few years ago, I lectured in a town in southern Germany about some of the treasures of wisdom in Christianity. Two clergymen were present who came up to me after the lecture and said they were really astonished at my positive attitude toward Christianity. They remarked that I had presented everything exactly the way it was supposed to be in Christianity. However, they felt my manner of presentation could be understood only by people with a certain amount of education, while their way of presenting Christianity was for all people and therefore the right way.

Well, I told them we must not judge on the basis of what pleases people; rather we are obligated to consider for our judgment only what corresponds to reality. People can easily delude themselves into believing that what they think is right. The less people are grounded in reality, the more they are usually convinced their opinion is right. Those who know the least about Christianity are often the very same ones who believe they know the most about it. In other words, it does not matter what we fool ourselves into thinking true; what matters is that we judge on the basis of reality.

So I asked the two clergymen whether everyone was still going to their churches, for that alone would decide the issue. The decisive point was not what these clergymen thought about Christianity but whether they were indeed speaking for all people, whether all people still went to their churches. They had to admit that indeed many people were staying away, unfortunately! Well, I told them that some of those people who didn't go to their churches anymore had come to hear my lecture, and I was speaking to them. For those who do not go to their churches are also seeking a way to the Mystery of Golgotha.

This way must be found. Our opinions must be dictated to us by reality, by what lives and works in reality, not by what we imagine. Obviously, everybody thinks his or her own method is the right one. But the right thing is not what we think is right, what we have thought out and have felt is right, but what reality reveals to us. Of course, that requires that we get used to immersing ourselves deeply into reality. It requires that we have the reverence for reality and devotion to it necessary to have our power of discernment, our sensitivity, and our feelings guided by reality. This is precisely what people have forgotten these days. They must learn it again in order to understand the smallest as well as the greatest things, to understand everyday life as well as what gives meaning to the whole earth evolution, that is, the Mystery of Golgotha.

## LECTURE SEVEN

July 18, 1916

# TOWARD IMAGINATION

WHEN WE look at the world around us as our senses and intellect perceive it, we have something we may call, metaphorically speaking, a great cosmic edifice. We form concepts, ideas, and images of what it is like and what goes on in it. What happens in this cosmic edifice, even down to the details, affects us so that we develop certain sympathies or antipathies for this or that, and these then are expressed in our feeling life. Prompted by our will we do this or that, and thus intervene in the processes going on in this cosmic edifice.

At first, people think that this building of the cosmos consists of separate parts, and so they study these parts and find them made up of still smaller parts, which they then examine, and so on. Finally, scientists arrive at what they call the smallest parts, the molecules and atoms. As I told you, nobody has ever seen these molecules and atoms; they are hypothetical—in a certain sense the hypothesis of their existence is justified, as long as we keep in mind that it is only a hypothesis. In short, we are to some extent justified in thinking that the cosmic building consists of parts or members, and there is nothing wrong with trying to get a clear picture of these. However, the people who give rein to their fantasy in thinking about the atom and who perhaps even talk about the life of the atom, or have still wilder notions about it—well, they are simply speaking about the nothing of a nothing, for the atom itself is merely hypothetical. To build a hypothesis upon other hypotheses is nothing else but building a house of cards; not even that, for in a house of cards we have at least the cards, but in speculations about the atom, we have nothing.

Based on the insights to be gained from spiritual science, people should admit that if they want to see more of the cosmic edifice than our senses perceive, they must arrive at a different perspective. They must come to a way of thinking that is as different from our thinking in everyday life (which is also that of ordinary science) as our usual, everyday way of thinking is from dreams. We dream in pictures, and we can have a whole world in these pictures of ours. Then we wake up and are no longer confronted with the pictures of our dreams but with realities that impinge upon us, that push and tug at us, demanding attention. We know this from life itself, not on the basis of a theory, for no theory can enable us to distinguish between dreams and so-called everyday reality. Only our direct experience of life can teach us this.

Now, it is also true that we can wake up from everyday life experiences, which we may call by analogy "a dream life," to a higher reality, the reality of the spirit. And again, it is only on the basis of life itself that we can distinguish between this higher spiritual reality and that of everyday life.

Now, what we see when we enter this world can be described with the following image—of course, one could use many different analogies to show the relationship between spiritual reality and ordinary reality, but I want to use a special image for this today. Let's imagine we are looking at a house built out of bricks. At first glance, the house appears to be composed of individual bricks. Of course, in the case of a house we can't go beyond the individual brick. However, let's assume the house doesn't consist of just ordinary bricks but of ones that are in turn extraordinarily artful constructions. Nevertheless, on first seeing the house we would only see the bricks, without having any idea that each brick in turn is a small work of art, so to speak. That is what happens in the case of the cosmic edifice.

We need only take one part of this cosmic edifice, the most complete one, let's say, the human being. Just think, as a part of this cosmic edifice, the human being seems to us to consist of parts: head, limbs, sense organs, and so on. We have tried over time to understand each part in its relation to the spiritual world. Remember, just recently I told you that the shape of our head can be traced to our previous earthly incarnation. The rest of our body, on the other hand, belongs to this incarnation and bears within it the rudiments of the head for the next life on earth.

I also spoke about the twelve senses and connected them with the twelve forces corresponding to the twelve signs of the zodiac. We said that microcosmically we bear within us the macrocosm with its forces working into us primarily from the twelve signs of the zodiac. Each of these forces is different: the forces of Aries differ from those of Taurus, which in turn differ from those of Gemini, and so on. Similarly, our eyes perceive different things than our ears. The twelve senses thus correspond to the twelve signs of the zodiac, but there is more to it than that.

We know that the rudiments of our sense organs were developed already on old Saturn, then evolved further during the old Sun and the old Moon periods up to the time of our earth. During our earth period, we have become self-enclosed beings with completely developed sense organs. In the Moon, Sun, and Saturn periods, human beings were much more open to the great cosmos, and the forces of the twelve signs of the zodiac affected the essential core of the human being. While the rudiments of our sense organs were being formed, they were affected by the forces of the zodiac. Thus, when we speak of the connection between the senses and the signs of the zodiac, we mean more than a mere correspondence. We seek those forces that have built our sense organs into us. We do not speak superficially of some vague kind of correspondence between the ego-sense and Aries or between the other senses and this or that sign of the zodiac.

We speak about this correspondence because during the earlier periods of our earthly planet the senses of the human being were not yet developed to the point of being enclosed in the organism. It was only through the twelve forces that the sense organs were built into our organism. We are built up out of the macrocosm, and when we study our sense organs, we are actually studying world-embracing forces that have worked in us over millions and millions of years, and have produced such wonderful parts of the human organism as the eyes and the ears. It is indeed true that we study these parts for their spiritual content, just as we would have to study each brick in order to examine the artistic structure of a house.

I could explain this with yet another image. Suppose we had some kind of structure artistically built up out of layers of paper rolls, some of them standing upright, others at an angle—all of these arranged artistically into some kind of a structure. Now imagine we had not just rolls of plain paper, but inside each roll a beautiful picture had been painted. Of course, just looking at the rolled up paper, we wouldn't see the paintings on the inside of the rolls. And yet, the paintings are there! And they must have been painted before the paper rolls were arranged in the artistic structure.

Now suppose it is not we who build up this artful structure of paper rolls, but the paper rolls have to form it by themselves. Of course, you can't imagine they could do this by themselves; nobody can imagine it. But let's suppose because the pictures are painted on all the paper rolls, the latter now have the power to arrange themselves in layers. And that gives you a picture of our true cosmic edifice. We can compare the paintings on the rolls with all that happened during the Saturn, Sun, and Moon periods, and is woven into every individual part of our cosmic building. These are not dead pictures, but living forces that build up everything meant to exist on earth. And we draw out what is artfully hidden in the structure made up of the individual rolls of the cosmic edifice—which science describes. This is what confronts us in our outer life. I have given much thought to finding an analogy corresponding as closely as possible to the facts of the matter and have come up with this image of the paper rolls with their living, active pictures. When you think this analogy through, you will find that when we first look at this structure, we cannot know anything about the paintings inside the rolls. If the structure is rather artful and ingenious, we can get an artful and ingenious description of it; however, it will not contain a word about the paintings inside the rolls.

You see, that's how it is with the conventional sciences. They describe this artistic structure, while ignoring completely the paintings on the inside of each roll. Now, you may wonder if a description of the elaborate structure of the rolls allows us to get an idea and to really know what is inside each roll as long as the rolls are rolled up and part of the whole structure? No, it does not! Conventional science is completely unable to arrive at the idea that the spiritual underlies our cosmic edifice. Therefore, simply continuing along the lines of conventional science will not lead to an understanding of spiritual science; something else must be added, something that has nothing to do with ordinary science.

Now picture all these layers of rolls; we can easily describe them and find them interesting and beautiful. Maybe some rolls are more slanted than others; maybe some are curved, and so on; all this can be nicely described. But in order to find out that there is a picture inside each roll, we will have to take out one of the paper rolls and unroll it. In other words, something special must be added to the human soul if we are to advance from the ordinary scientific outlook to that of the science of the spirit. The soul must be taken hold of by something of a special nature. This is what is so difficult to understand for our materialist culture. Yet, this must be understood again as it was in earlier cultural epochs when a spiritual world view permeated the physical one. In ancient times, people were always aware that everything they had to know about the spiritual content of the world was based on the spiritual taking hold of the soul. That is why people back then spoke not only about science, but also about initiation and the like.

Another analogy, one taken from the ancient traditions of spiritual science, will make the matter completely clear to you if you think it through. In spiritual science we speak of an "occult reading of the world," and rightly so. What conventional science is doing cannot be called "reading the world." If you look at what is written on a page of some book or other publication and you can't read at all, then what is written there will of course remain completely incomprehensible to you. Still, you could describe the handwriting; you could describe the lines, loops, and crossbars; you could tell what the individual letters look like and how they are combined. It will be a nice description, not unlike the one contemporary science gives of outer physical reality or the one contemporary history provides. However, this is not the same as reading.

Obviously, people do not learn to read by taking a page from a book, without having any idea what it means to read, and trying to figure out the meaning of the text from the shape of the letters. Reading is taught in childhood. We learn to read not by describing the shape of the letters, but because something spiritual is conveyed to us, and we are mentally and spiritually stimulated to read. It is the same with everything we call the higher and lower degrees of initiation. Initiation was not based on teaching souls to describe what was outside them, but on teaching them to read it, to decipher, so to speak, the meaning of the world. Thus, it was with good reason that what is spiritual in the world was called "the Word," for the world has to be read if it is to be understood spiritually. And we do not learn to read by memorizing the shape of the letters but by receiving spiritual impulses.

That is what I want to make clear through the presentations in our circles. As you remember the themes running through our lectures, you will see I have always tried to use images. Today I am also using them, for it is only through images that one can lead the way into the spiritual. As soon as images are crammed into concepts applying only to the physical plane, they no longer contain what they should. This confuses people because they cannot grasp what is given in images in such a way that it is a true reality for them. Right away, they think of the images themselves in completely materialistic terms. When we look at more primitive cultures, we see that people then did not have our modern concepts but thought in images and expressed their reality in them. Even in Asian cultures, which are somewhat atavistic because they have kept features from earlier times, you find that to meaningfully express something profound, people always speak in images, images that definitely have the significance of a reality.

Let us take an example where the image really has the significance of an immediate reality, of a coarse and rough reality, so to speak. Europeans frequently find it very hard to understand Asians who have preserved older, atavistic ideas of reality; they often have only a very rough understanding of Asians. There is a very beautiful Asian novella telling the following story.

Once upon a time there was a couple, and they had a daughter. The daughter grew up and was sent to school in the capital because she showed special talents. On leaving school, she married a merchant, an acquaintance of her father. She had a son and died when the boy was four years old. The day after the mother's funeral, the child suddenly said: "Mother has gone upstairs to the top floor, and she must be there now!" And the whole family went upstairs.

Now we must put ourselves into the Asian soul in order to understand what follows. I am telling you something bordering closely on reality. Yet if a European were told by a four-year-old that his mother, who had been buried the day before, was upstairs and if he were then to go up with a candle to look around, he would of course find nothing there. The whole thing would be denied. In other words, we have to try to put ourselves into the Asian mind.

Well, the family went up there with a light and found the mother actually standing there before a dresser and staring at it. All the drawers were closed, and the people felt that there had to be something in the dresser that was troubling her. They emptied the drawers and took the items that had been in them to the temple to store them there. In that way those things would be removed from the world. They believed that now the soul would not return anymore; they knew it would return only if something was still binding it to this world.

However, the soul returned anyway! Every evening when the family looked upstairs, she was there. Finally, the family went to a wise guardian of the temple; he came, said he must be left undisturbed, and recited his sutras. And, when the "hour of the rat" struck—in the Orient, the time between midnight and two in the morning is called the hour of the rat—there was the woman again, staring at a certain spot on the dresser. He asked her if anything was there, and she gave him to understand by a gesture that there was indeed something. He opened the first drawer but nothing was in it, the second, nothing, the third, nothing, the fourth and still nothing. Then it occurred to him to lift up the paper lining of the drawers, and there between the last layer of paper and the bottom of the drawer he found a letter. He promised to tell nobody about this letter and to burn it in the temple. He did so, and the soul never returned again.

Now this oriental story actually agrees with reality; it expresses reality. It would be very difficult to present this matter in European concepts. Besides, the conceptions of modern Europeans are still too coarse. They think when something is real, then everybody must be able to see it. Europeans generally allow only for two things; either everyone sees something, and then it is a reality, or not everyone sees it, and then it is subjective and not objective. Now this distinction between subjective and objective applies only to the physical world but has no meaning in the spiritual world. There we cannot call anything others do not see subjective but not objective.

Now you may say that such things as told in that story also exist in Europe. Indeed, they do, but Europeans are generally glad to say it is only fiction and is not necessarily true. That is why it is so much easier to speak about the spiritual world in fiction. Fiction does not lay any claim to truth. People are content when they do not have to believe what is said in stories and the like. However, the objection that this is after all only a novella does not count. Europeans obviously have little understanding of Asians or they would not say such things. What Europeans call novellas, or art, is a most superfluous and useless game to Asians and means nothing to them. They even make fun of our telling stories about things that do not exist. Asians do not understand this. In what they call works of art, they tell only about what really exists, albeit in the spiritual world. That is the profound difference between the European and the Asian world views.

That Europeans write novellas about things that do not exist is, according to the Oriental view, a highly superfluous activity. In their view, all our art is only a rather superfluous and useless occupation. Clearly, we have to understand the Asian art works we possess as Imaginations of spiritual reality; otherwise we will never understand them at all. We Europeans in turn judge Asian stories not by Asian standards but by our own and call them fanciful and beautiful fiction, products of the fertile, unbridled Oriental imagination.

People will gradually have to realize that we have to speak more and more in images. Of course, if we were to speak in pictures only, we would be going against modern

European culture; so we can't do that. But we can gradually allow ordinary thinking, applicable only on the physical plane, to turn into thinking about the spiritual world, and then into pictorial thinking, which develops under the influence of the spiritual world. Natural scientists also develop a view of the world, but if they think their view is clear and comprehensible, they make the same mistake as we would if we claimed we could paint a portrait, and the subject would then step out of the canvas and walk around the room.

In my latest book, *Vom Menschenrätsel*, I move from the usual logical presentation to a pictorial one.[1] This has to become our general style of presentation if spiritual science is really to become a part of Western civilization. A philosophical treatise about the same matters would cite innumerable logical arguments, would turn the most elaborate and artificial phrases; yet it would be virtually dead. It would aim only at understanding the outer layering of the rolls, not what lives as paintings on the inside of each roll. These things become meaningful only when we apply them in our lives, for that is how we learn to understand life. So-called logical proofs have to be imbued with life before we can understand spiritual science in a living way.

As you know, some people are musical and others are not, and there is a very great difference between those who are musical and those who are not. In terms of the soul a musical person is quite different from an unmusical one. I do not mean this as a criticism of unmusical people; it is simply a statement of fact. Those who look more closely at life may perhaps not go so far as to agree with Shakespeare's statement, "The man that hath no music in himself . . . .
Is fit for such treasons, stratagems and spoils. . . .
Let no such man be trusted."[2]

Though we may not arrive right away at that conclusion, there is a certain difference in the souls of musical and unmusical persons.

Now, you may want to know why there are musical and unmusical people. If you look for an answer in psychology, which follows along the lines of the natural sciences, I do not think you will find much that could cast a light on this question. If psychology were to explain why one person is musical and another is not, if it were to deal with such subtleties, then it would finally do some good.

However, there is yet another difference between human beings. We find people who go through life and are, in a sense, hardly touched by what goes on around them. Others go through life with so open a soul that they are deeply affected by what is going on around them. They feel deep joy over some things and suffer over others; they feel happiness about some things and sadness about others. There are those who are dulled to impressions and those who are sensitive and empathize with all the world. There are people who shortly after entering a room that is not too crowded have a certain rapport with the others, because they can feel very quickly what the others feel by way of so-called imponderables. On the other hand, there are individuals who come into contact with many people but do not really get to know a single one of them because they do not have the gift I have just described. They judge others by what they themselves are, and when these others are different from them, they really consider them more or less bad people.

Still, there are those who give their time and attention to others, sharing their experiences. As a rule these are people who can also empathize with animals, with beetles and sparrows, who can feel joy with some events and sorrow with others. Notice how often this happens in life, especially at a certain age; young people are happy about all kinds of things. They are up one minute and down the next, while other people call them stupid because, to their minds, nothing really matters much anyway. So, there exist these two types of people. Of course, the two qualities are sometimes more and sometimes less developed; they are not necessarily very pronounced but are still clearly noticeable.

Now, the spiritual scientist, trying to understand the world from his point of view, comes to the conclusion that those people are musical in this life who empathized with everything and moved easily from joy to sorrow and from sorrow to joy in their previous life. This was internalized, and that is how the rhythmical flexibility of the musical soul developed. On the other hand, people who were dulled in their sensitivity to outer events in the preceding incarnation do not become musical. Nevertheless, they may have other excellent qualities, may even have been great world reformers and have influenced world history.

Imagine a person living in Rome at the time when Michelangelo and Raphael produced their great works and not seeing anything but immorality in the Rome of that time. Now Rome was indeed immoral and decadent. But this individual ignored everything that was not immoral, for instance, the art of Michelangelo and Raphael. Perhaps he became a very important personality, a reformer who accomplished great things. What I am telling you is not meant as malicious criticism. Still, people are unmusical because in the previous incarnation they did not receive vivid impressions of things that do deeply impress other souls.

Think how transparent life would become and how well we would be able to understand others if we approached them with such knowledge. And when we keep in mind that spiritual science imbues our souls with a longing to perceive in pictures, then all this should seem to us something desirable.

Of course, if everything were limited to concepts and if spiritual science were to dissect everyone and investigate what the person was like in previous incarnations, then people would do well to be on their guard against spiritual science. No one would venture forth among people anymore if they would analyze like this. However, this would happen only if we worked with crude concepts. If we stay with pictures, the latter lay hold of our feelings, and we arrive at an emotional understanding of others, which we do not need to transform into concepts. We turn it into concepts only when we express it as a general truth. It is quite all right to talk about the flexibility of the soul in a preceding incarnation and musicality in a later one, as I have done, but it would be in poor taste if I were to approach a person who is musical and describe what he or she was like in the previous incarnation based on this talent. These truths are derived from individual details, but the point is not to apply them to details. This must be understood in the deepest sense.

Most people may understand truths like these, but when we go a bit further, then what is meant to enlighten humanity can easily lead to nonsense. For example, we often speak about reincarnation in general terms, and at one time, I talked to one of our branch groups about the relationship between reincarnation and self-knowledge, a theme that deserves some attention. I said it would be good to try to apply certain concepts we acquire from spiritual science to our efforts to understand ourselves. I explained that at the beginning of our life karma often brings us into contact with people who were connected with us at about the middle of our previous life, when we were in our thirties. In other words, we are not right away with the people we were with at the corresponding time in our earlier incarnation. This is how I have explained various rules of reincarnation; you can also find in my lectures how reincarnation can be applied to self-knowledge. Well, what did all this lead to in those days? It turned out that shortly thereafter a number of people founded a sort of "Club of the Reincarnated." Yes, indeed, there was a clique that explained who each member had been in the preceding incarnation or even in all previous lives. Of course they had all been exceedingly eminent figures in human history, that goes without saying, and they had all been connected in their earlier lives.

That was a nuisance for a long time. Naturally this is all terrible because it violates what I have emphasized, namely, that if you are to know anything about your previous incarnation, in our era you will not understand it from within yourself. Rather, your attention will be drawn to it through some outer event or through another person. In our time it is generally false when somebody looks within and then claims to have been this or that person. If we are to know anything, it will be told to us from outside.

Those who founded the "Club of the Reincarnated" would have had to wait a long time before being told about their previous incarnations. Yet they had all been important personalities, the most important in human history! When the thing became known, and those people were asked why they had done all this, they answered that they did it because I had said in a lecture one should cultivate self-knowledge in the light of reincarnation. Since then they had all been busy thinking about who they had been in previous lives and how they had been connected with each other.

In such a case we sin against the reverence we should have for the great spiritual truths. This reverence consists in staying appropriately with the image, with the metaphor;

only when it is really necessary should the picture be left behind, and should we go beyond the metaphor. In spiritual science we have to develop reverence and to realize that this sophistry, this putting things into the concept, is always a bad thing. It is always bad to think about spiritual matters in the same way we think about things on the physical plane. Indeed, when we acquire this reverence, we also develop certain moral qualities, which cannot unfold if we don't carry all this in our soul in the right way. Accordingly, spiritual science will also lead to a moral uplifting of our modern culture.

Now we Europeans say—and rightly so—that because we can see the Christ Mystery in our spiritual life, we have an advantage over other cultures, for example, over the Asian or oriental ones. What those cultures know about the spiritual does not include the Christ Being. The Japanese, Chinese, Hindus, Persians, do not include the Christ Being in their thinking about the spiritual interrelationships in the world. We are therefore right in calling the Asian world view atavistic, a relic of an earlier age. Though those people may have an exceedingly lofty understanding of the world, as, for instance, in the Vedanta philosophy, their inability to understand the Christ Mystery makes their world view an atavistic one. To be able to penetrate deeply into certain connections is not necessarily a sign of great spiritual heights.

For example, I used to know a man who was among us for a long time and even belonged to the "Club of the Reincarnated," and he propounded excellent theories about certain conditions of life on Atlantis. Continuing along the lines of my book on Atlantis, this person came to very interesting conclusions that were true. Yet, he was so loosely connected to our movement that he left it when external reasons made it convenient for him to do so. Under certain conditions, it takes only a particular formation of the etheric body to see into supersensible regions. However, if spiritual science is to flow in a living way into our culture, it has to take hold of the whole person so that he or she can grow close to its deepest impulses. And then spiritual science will create what our culture, which is developing more and more into a materialistic one, is lacking.

Thus, we are right in saying we have the advantage of the Christ Mystery over the Asian cultures. But what do Asians say about this? Now, I am not telling you something I just made up; I am telling you what the more reasonable Asians really say. They agree we have the advantage of the Christ Mystery over them. They say, "That is something we do not have, and that's why you Europeans think you are on a higher stage of cultural development. However, you also say, 'By their fruits ye shall know them,' and your religion tells you to love one another. But when we look at how you live, it does not seem as though you are doing that. You send missionaries to us in Asia who tell us all kinds of great things; however, when we come to Europe, we find people do not at all live as they should if all we've been told were true." Well, that's what the Asians say.

Now just think whether they are so entirely wrong. At a religious convention where people from all religions were to speak, this case was discussed, and the Asian representatives said what I have just told you. They said, "You send us missionaries, which is very nice. However, you have had Christianity for two thousand years now, and we cannot see that it has advanced your moral development so much beyond ours."

There are good reasons for this, my dear friends. You see, Asians live much more in the group-soul and much less as individuals. Morals are in a sense innate to them, inborn through the group-soul. Europeans, precisely because they are developing their I, must leave the group-soul behind and must be left to their own resources. That is why egoism inevitably had to appear. It goes hand in hand with individualism. People will only gradually be able to come together again by understanding Christianity in a higher sense.

Much has prevented those who have thought about Christianity, even the best of them, from truly understanding the consequences of the Mystery of Golgotha. Granted, it is certainly very "profound" to say we must experience the Christ in our own inner being. You see, there is what I would like to call a symbolical theosophy. As you know, I have always spoken out against this theosophy that wants to explain everything as symbols. It explains even the resurrection of Christ as merely an inner experience even though in reality it is a historical event. Christ really did rise again in the world, but many a theosophist finds it easier to deal with the matter by claiming it is merely an inner process. As you know, this was the special skill of the late Franz Hartmann; in every lecture he repeatedly explained theosophy to his audience by saying that one has to understand oneself inwardly, to comprehend God in oneself, and so on.[3]

Now if you understand the Gospels properly, you will not find any grounds for the idea that the Gospels advocate people should experience the Christ only inwardly. There are theosophical symbolists who reinterpret various passages, but in reality everything in the Gospels confirms the truth of the great word, "Where two or three are gathered together in My name, there am I in the midst of them." The Christ is a social phenomenon. The Christ passed through the Mystery of Golgotha as a reality, and He is here as a reality, belonging not to the individual but to the common life of all people. What He does is what is important. These things can often be better understood in pictures than in abstract concepts.

Just recently we went to see a friend on leave from the front lines of the battlefield, where he has since returned. This friend was kind enough to get us a taxicab, and when he returned with it and pulled up, he told us he had had a conversation with the driver. This driver was an altogether peculiar man, for when we had arrived and were about to get out, he opened the door and after he had been paid, he gave us two little pamphlets called "Peace Messenger." He was making propaganda for the spiritual world while working his job! Then our friend told us that this driver had told him the essential thing is for people to find the Christ, everything depends on the Christ. In other words, our friend had picked out a cab at the taxistand and gotten into a conversation with the driver, who told him the world will advance only when people find the Christ, whom they have not yet found.

Well, the cab driver added a few other things and said, "You see, with Christ it's like this. Just think, I am a very respectable man, an exemplary man, and I have children who are all good for nothing. But am I any less respectable and exemplary a man because I have children who are no good? They all know me, or think they know me, but they are still good-for-nothings. That's how I think of the Christ. He belongs to us all, He is the person we all look to but that does not mean everybody necessarily really understands Him."

This cab driver has created a marvelous picture of the special life of Christ, of His isolated life! He has discovered that Christ is living among us, living with us, belonging to us all and not to any one individual. He saw his sons who were all no good as the individuals, who were good for nothing and would have to struggle before reaching an understanding. If this cab driver had wanted to express this extraordinarily significant idea in philosophical terms, nothing would have come of it. But his picture reflects wonderfully what we are trying to understand. Of course, such a picture is not quite sufficient; an individual may understand it, but you will not influence our culture with it. I just wanted to show you that even the simplest soul can light on a true picture. This is how things should really flow into pictures. I have tried to achieve this particularly in the style of my latest book, which deals with nontheosophical matters. However, in its presentation this book is "theosophical," if we want to use that expression.

It is important to understand our teachings more and more between the lines, so to speak, if we want to grasp correctly that they have to become life, the life of each one of us. And what weighs so heavily upon one's soul is just this awful difficulty of integrating these things into life.

You see, if these things are important to you, and particularly if you really know our rationalist culture, you will realize that what pulsates through spiritual science has to live in all branches of culture. It must influence thinking, feeling, and willing, only then will it fulfill its mission. To feel connected with our cause really takes quite some inner strength. It is a pity that it takes such an infinitely long time for people to feel thoroughly connected with the impulses of spiritual science. In the meantime, we can see people passing by and ignoring precisely what they should be focusing on.

Now let me tell you about another case. There was a very learned gentleman who used to be a member of our Society; in fact, he was tremendously learned, but his erudition did not satisfy him. He was profoundly unhappy in spite of all his learning, which included a knowledge of oriental languages and the culture of the Near East. Now this man came and asked for advice. In such a case my advice will necessarily have to show that through an understanding of spiritual science the spirit can enter into a science such as oriental philosophy. So I indicated that he should permeate all this scholarly material with what he had received from spiritual science. However, for him the two things merely continued to exist side by side. On the one hand, he pursued his oriental studies as this is done in the universities; on the other hand, he pursued spiritual science. The two never came together for him; he could not permeate the one with the other.

Now just think how fruitful it would be if someone who knows so much—and this man did indeed know a tremendous amount—were to take his science and learning and imbue it with theosophy! He wouldn't even have to let it be known that he thinks theosophically if he feared people might look askance at him for that. Still, he could then present all this in his university lectures. That man could very well have penetrated the culture on the Euphrates and the Tigris and the one a bit further west—he was particularly at home in Egyptology—with spiritual science and could have accomplished something remarkable. In any case, he could have achieved something more fruitful than the popularizing stuff produced by our common writers. Recently a piece by such a popular writer appeared in a widely read daily paper. The fellow had written an article on the discovery of a sphinxlike figure during construction for the Baghdad railway—well, even if his name is Arthur Bonus, he is still definitely not a "good one!"[4] This article is absolutely terrible!

The ideal we have in mind, my dear friends, is to let our thinking be carried by what spiritual science gives us. And it should be the same in life too, in our everyday life with each other. Spiritual science can be carried into everything. If we did not intend this, did not have this ideal, then spiritual science would not be able to bear fruit. The challenge to make it fruitful meets us everywhere.

Just think, there are excellent historians who write about the history of England at the time of James I, let's say.[5] Then there are excellent historians who write books about the life of Francisco Suarez, the Jesuit.[6] As you know, I have to be careful what I say when I speak about Jesuitism. That is, I must not say too much that is positive—or at least what can be misunderstood as positive. Nevertheless, it is true that most people know about this Suarez only that in one of his writings he is supposed to have explicitly preached regicide. But this is not true. In general, people often know things that are untrue but don't as often and as thoroughly know things that are true.

Now, excellent books about this Suarez are available nowadays; most of them are written by Jesuits. You can read these books about Suarez, the successor of Ignatius of Loyola, and understand them.[7] That does not mean that you will become, or have been, a Jesuit, nor that you have to put up with people drawing such conclusions. The facts are clear, and when we connect them, we can answer one of biggest questions of modern history. These two individuals, James I and Francisco Suarez, the Jesuit philosopher, are complete opposites. At the time of James I, a very ahrimanic new development was inaugurated. Another development began with Suarez that was very luciferic. Their combined influence, and particularly their fights against each other, shaped much of what lives and weaves in the present age.

Here we come to mysterious connections. I don't want to blame anyone with what I am going to say now. For example, we find that a great deal of what these days is called historical materialism or Marxism, the Social Democratic outlook, can be traced directly to Suarez. Now please do not take this to mean that I am saying the Social Democrats are Jesuits. Nevertheless, there are in a certain sense good reasons for connecting the Social Democrats with the Jesuits. By the same token, many members of the opposing party, that is, those who oppose social democracy, can be traced back directly to what was inaugurated by James I.

With this, I have indicated something that lives in many people's thoughts. Particularly in occult communities you find two main streams, and from these flows something that is not occult. These two main streams produce two typical, contrasting figures: James I of England, in whom an extraordinary initiate-soul lived, and Suarez.

Now, if you read the biography of Suarez, you will not understand it at all if you have not really grasped spiritual science. Suarez was one of those people who are at first bad students and don't learn anything. According to the contemporary materialist view, such people are hopeless cases and not good for anything. However, one can easily prove that many great geniuses did not learn anything when they were in school. Well, Suarez was also one of the bad students, and even in college he was not yet what one might call a bright man. Then all of a sudden he changed, and every biography of him describes this sudden awakening. The gift of brilliance suddenly awakened in him, and he wrote extraordinarily interesting books, which are, unfortunately, not widely known. This happened all of a sudden, kindled by some of the things I told you about in my lectures on the spiritual exercises of the Jesuits, which Suarez also practiced. Through these he awakened something in himself that enabled him to develop special mental and spiritual forces.

Thus, the biography of Suarez proves—as it can also be proved in the case of James I—that he turned around, so to speak, and came from the unspiritual into the spiritual. This soul, which later achieved outstanding accomplishments, was born at a certain moment. Its development did not proceed in a straight line, but took place in a sudden jolt, produced either by karma or by an influence on the person in question that can be compared to how we learn to read in elementary school: not by describing the shape of the letters, but by receiving an impulse through which we learn to understand the letters.

Here, you see again how spiritual science can guide us in understanding these historical connections, and then we can see life quite differently. If you take in spiritual science in a living way, then your attitude to life really changes, and you can think of other things to do than what you have been doing. It is hard to imagine that a person who takes in spiritual science in a living way could come up with the strange idea, for example, that he or she is Mary Magdalene reincarnated. This would not occur to such a person; instead he or she would focus on other contents of the soul.

It is hard to have to watch how slowly the development in the direction I indicated proceeds. People really take spiritual science far too much as merely a theory or as simply something to be enjoyed. However, it must be studied in a living way. Now that we are together before parting for some time at the beginning of summer, when we will have to return to Dornach, I would like to discuss briefly a few important points we must consider in this regard.

You see, my dear friends, if things had turned out as many

people adhering to older traditions had expected at the time when we first established spiritual science here fourteen years ago, we would have become a sect. For all the ideas brought over from England were headed toward the formation of a sect. And many people felt very comfortable being completely secluded in their small circles. Then they could call the other people outside their circles fools. There was very little control over this. However, this kind of thing had to stop.

Spiritual science has to reckon with our whole culture. We have always considered this culture, and we have emphasized particularly in public lectures what one can get into European heads these days—regardless of how many objections were raised. Now I don't want to criticize—that would be silly—but still, we have to understand that our movement really must not become a sect and must not even have any characteristics of a sectarian movement if it is to fulfill its task. We can accomplish much if we take the general culture into account. People outside our movement for the most part write nonsense about it—if they write about it at all. You may say this does not matter in a deeper sense. On the contrary, it matters very much! That is why we have to defend ourselves and do what we can to stop it. We have to do everything possible so that eventually people will not write nonsense but something better.

However, in a spiritual sense it is even more harmful when what was intended only for members of our immediate circle is brought in the wrong way before the public so that our lecture cycles are now sold in second-hand bookshops. Granted, we may not be able to prevent this. Still it happens again and again, not only that our lecture cycles can be bought in second-hand bookshops but other equally detrimental things as well. For instance, somebody just recently told me about a person he had worked with for a long time. He said that person did not write anything on his own initiative but belongs to a somewhat dubious clique, which has complete control over him. He himself only sits down and goes ahead with his writing. Now this person has written many brochures about our spiritual science and even big books. In those you find not only quotations from my printed and published works, but also long passages from the cycles. In other words, it is not just that one can buy these cycles in second-hand bookshops, but, in fact, anyone wanting to write a stupid book these days is able to get hold of them. Such people then buy two or three cycles and copy passages that sound completely absurd when taken out of context, and then they can make a book out of all that.

These are the problems that result from our having to face the public while at the same time being a Society. However, we have to understand this problem if we want to overcome it. As I said, I do not want to criticize, for that would be totally useless; instead, I want to describe the problem. I want to show you where the difficulties lie, and we just have to watch for them. In the immediate future even more abominable things will be done against our Society than we have had to endure up to now. We won't be able to change that in the twinkling of an eye. Still, we must not ignore both the encouraging, pleasant elements and the annoying ones in the way the world judges our movement as though we were trying to become totally unmusical in the next incarnation.

You see, those who think purely egoistically—as I said, this is not meant as criticism, but merely as description—think that spiritual science has more to say about certain relationships in nature than ordinary science. Thus, people turn to me for medical advice even though I have emphasized repeatedly that I am only a teacher or cultivator of spiritual science, and not a physician. Of course, people may want some friendly advice and to refuse that would be absurd. If people come for friendly advice, why should it be denied them even if it concerns matters of natural science? However, after everything that has happened, I have to request that nobody seeks my advice on medical matters who is not in the care of a physician. People who think selfishly do not consider that such things are not permissible nowadays and that they bring us into conflict with the world around us, and that is detrimental to our spiritual science. We have to make an effort to improve things; we have to advocate everywhere that there should be more than just the officially authorized medicine, which is based on pure materialism. We can certainly do this, but we must not just selfishly think of what is good for us individually if this could interfere with what our movement must be.

Spiritual science can give advice, and it would be absurd if it didn't. It would be pathetic indeed if one could not give some advice to a person suffering from this or that ailment. However, it is a great risk to give advice when the following happens—and I am telling you a true story here. Someone was ill in a town where I had just previously said that I definitely do not want people to turn to me in case of illness. I had said so publicly and officially. Now, someone became ill and was admitted into a sanitarium, where he remained for some time. A long-standing member of ours who had always been connected with the most intimate aspects of our cause wrote to this sanitarium, explaining that the patient in question could now be discharged because Dr. Steiner gave such and such advice. The member wrote this to the physician, who replied that this just goes to show we don't mean it when we claim theosophy wants to be nothing but theosophy and does not want to meddle in other people's business.

Yes, indeed, my dear friends, we have to pay attention to such things. If we ignore them, it will not be for the good of the movement. Of course, this is only one case, but variations of this are happening again and again. This leads to a peculiar feature of our movement, about which I have to speak now. What I am referring to is that the new good side of our movement comes to light less rapidly than other new developments that have also never before been there. They prove that our movement is indeed something new; however, these are peculiar novelties.

For example, let us suppose this or that were written in my published books. If no cycles were getting into the wrong hands, people outside our movement would refute what is in my books. Well, let them do it, but then they would present *their* opinion. It would never occur to people out there who do not belong to our Society to copy sentences from my books to prove I am a "bad guy." No one would do this; instead people out there would present their own opinions. What happens in our Society, however, is that someone accepts our teaching—swallows it hook, line, and sinker, as the saying goes—but then refutes me with my own teaching. You can see an example of this in an as yet unpublished exposition.

As you may remember, in an earlier edition of *Riddles of Philosophy*—the book then was called *Views of Life and World in the Nineteenth Century*—I explained that Leverrier discovered the planet Neptune merely on the basis of his calculations about Uranus, before Neptune had been seen.[8] Neptune was first seen at the Berlin observatory, but its existence was already known earlier simply because of calculations. I referred to this example to show that something may follow from calculations, that we can know of a fact merely on the basis of our thinking.

Well, just recently someone wrote that he has applied this very obvious and convincing idea, but in a different field. He claims to have found that something is wrong in our movement, that there are disruptions and interferences like the ones Leverrier found in observing the planet Uranus. If Uranus does not move the way it should according to calculations based on the general laws of gravity, then obviously something is interfering. Similarly, according to this individual, something supposedly interferes with our movement. So he propounds the hypothesis that there is something disruptive here, interfering with everything. And then, in the same way Leverrier discovered Neptune, this individual discovered that the evil interferences in our movement are in me. As the astronomers in the observatory here turned their telescope to the place where Neptune was said to be, so this person focused his spiritual telescope on me and found the evil there.

This is a special case; the methods I have given are all applied to my character and I am refuted with myself. In this man's circle a letter was written recently—not by him but by others from his circle—saying that I have no right to complain about this refutation because I myself had always said spiritual science was the common property of everyone and that it would be wrong to think spiritual science originated with the spiritual investigator. Well now, when things get this confused, there can be no simple, clear explanation for them. This, indeed, is something new arising in our Society. Outside, where the old still holds good, others are refuted by means of what the critics themselves think. But within our Society people do not take their own thoughts, but what they read in the lecture cycles and use it against me.

For example, in the letter I mentioned you can find many quotations from my book *An Outline of Occult Science* and others.[9] Everywhere you'll find exhortations to read this or that for yourself so you'll see I am actually an evil, bad guy. Now, the letter does not claim what I say is bad. On the contrary, because it is good, it can be used as evidence. This is something entirely new arising in our midst, a novelty based on the theory that our teaching can be accepted and then used to slander the one who is trying to popularize it. That is indeed something new!

This may be a particularly blatant case; still, on a smaller scale such things occur very frequently. If we so much as say anything about such things, then we get threats! Recently a letter informed us that articles and pamphlets, whose titles constitute a direct threat, would soon appear in shop windows and newspapers. As I said, if we dare make a sound, this is what happens. This is a novelty, something new in our movement, and we must pay attention to it.

We can see difficulties cropping up before they have fully emerged, so to speak, for we can predict what will happen. Tell me, should we really never talk about such a case as the one I have mentioned; should we always keep quiet about it? That is certainly possible. However, since the members themselves are not trying to discover such things, nobody in our circles would ever find out. Therefore, we must speak about it. But what happens when we speak about it? Pretty soon you will probably read in another letter—of course, this is just a hypothesis for now—that I have been speaking about a private letter before a large number of members. And this is simply because there are certainly people here who will immediately report somewhere or other what I have said tonight. That is happening all the time. Not talking about these things is no good, but talking about them only encourages what is repeatedly being done. We can predict the outcome.

I do not want to criticize; I only want to point out that in a movement where spiritual science lives, that is, where occult things pulsate, difficulties do indeed arise, and we must pay attention to them. If we ignore them, they will continue and get worse. Yes, we have to be prepared for the attacks to get more and more trenchant. If we were a small sect, this would not be the case. But our movement had to become just what it has become, and so that's the way it is.

Much of what comes from outside is understandable although many attacks ostensibly from the outside actually can be proven to have originated within our circles. Just today we have learned that in Dornach we practice eurythmy, which supposedly consists in dancing to the point of reaching a trance, as the dervishes do, and so on. We were told this news was reported by members. Members have reported that we dance until we reach a state of trance! In reality this was told to one of our members by people totally unconnected with us, but these people said they had heard it from members whose names they mentioned.

These difficulties come up because we have united spiritual science and the Society, and we must examine them carefully. If we ignore them, we cannot progress properly and we risk the dissolution of our Society and its total annihilation. True, all this does not harm spiritual science as such, but it does harm what spiritual science is also trying to be. It is harmful when people come and tell me that much of what they read about spiritual science interested them, but then they sat at a table in a boarding house and heard a lady prattle on about theosophy and say all kinds of things, and, of course, they feel they cannot join a Society where such a lot of rubbish is talked that's supposed to be theosophy. Now, this is not an isolated case; this happens again and again in one way or another.

Speaking about these things at the end of a serious talk may be misunderstood. However, it is absolutely necessary, my dear friends, that you know about them and pay attention to them. Our Society must be the carrier and helper of spiritual science; however, it can easily develop in such a way that it works against what spiritual science is to bring to world evolution. Naturally, in the individual case it is easy to understand that much of this damage could not be prevented. Yet we can be sure that the damage will look quite different if we pay attention to it and if we ourselves try to keep to a certain line, a certain direction, so to speak. Sometimes it is indeed extremely difficult, but also necessary, to take a hard line in a certain direction. Then novelties like the ones I just described will be rightly judged. It does not happen anywhere else that a person is refuted with his own works, for the idea of accepting a person's teaching in order to refute him with them is in itself absurd and foolish. Of course, if someone talks nonsense, you can use his nonsense against him, but that is not the point here. Rather, the new twist here is that the teaching is accepted and the person is refuted on the basis of his teaching.

On a smaller scale, things like that are very widespread. And they are not far removed from another evil I will also speak about before coming to a close. Indeed, it happens nowhere else as often as in our movement that somebody does something one can condemn, in fact, has to condemn. Then people take sides. For example, somebody may say something against the leading personalities in our Society, or against long-standing members, or against the *Vorstand*, as we unfortunately have to call it. Yet, even if the allegations are completely unfounded and perhaps only made up, clearly revealing the accuser's underlying motivation, you will rarely find that people try to discover whether the unfortunate *Vorstand* is right. Instead, people immediately take sides with the person who is wrong.

In fact, that is the rule here: people take sides with those who are wrong, and write letters asking the victims of the attack to do something to preserve the friendship, to straighten things out again—after all, one must show love. When somebody commits an unkind deed against another, people do not write to the one who did the deed. Instead, they write to the one who suffered it that he should show some kindness and that it would be very unloving not to do something to set things right again. It never occurs to them to ask this of the one who is wrong. Such peculiar things happen in our circle.

Of certain other things we will not even speak; nevertheless, there may of course come a time when we have to speak about them too. Today, we wanted to talk about a serious topic since we are living in a serious time and our movement is to influence it in a serious way. Still, we absolutely had to point out these peculiar things. You must pay attention to them, for things are indeed happening that you will find hard to believe if you hear about them. Nevertheless, we constantly have to deal with such things, and nobody should misunderstand that I had to speak about them; instead you should all reflect on them a bit.

It is our intention not to have as long a break between lectures as we had in the past. We may be able to meet again in fall; however, it is better not to promise anything specific in this time of uncertainties and obstacles. And so I ask you to use the picture I have tried to paint in this winter of our souls and to let your souls dwell on it during this summer. Bring to life in your souls, in a kind of meditation, what we have talked about and reflect on the basic requirements for the integration of our spiritual science into the general culture.[10]

And so let us now part, my dear friends, in the realization that we can do much to help integrate what we take seriously into our times if we are all really committed to it. People now sacrifice much more than ever before in such numbers and in so short a time. We are living in a hard time, a time of suffering. May the hardships and sufferings also be a summons to us. No matter how difficult it may be to incorporate the spiritual into human evolution, it has to happen. However much or however little we can do as individuals, let us do it! Let us try to understand the right way to do our part so that what cannot come about of itself but has to be done through people will result. Of course, there will also be help from the spiritual world. Thus, let us remain united in thoughts like this even when we will be apart for a while. People who are united in spirit are always together. Neither space nor time can separate them, and particularly not a more or less short span of time. Let us remain united in thoughts that try again to penetrate a little bit what I have said here in these days to your souls.

We must take in the full weight of the significance of the truths connected with the Mystery of Golgotha. Let us realize that in order to understand this or that we have to be in the solitude of our souls and return there again and again. But let us also understand that we belong to humanity and that the One Who went through the Mystery of Golgotha brought something from spiritual heights to the earth for all human beings, for the working together of all people. And let us remember that He said: "When two or three are gathered together in My Name, there am I in their midst."

Through all we experience in solitude we can prepare ourselves for what the Christ is destined to be to the world through us. But Christ is in our midst only if we try to carry into the world what we strive for in solitude, and we can do that only if we understand the conditions for carrying it into the world. Let us look at these conditions! Let us open our eyes, and, above all, let us have the courage to admit that things are as they are and must be dealt with accordingly.

When I speak here about Christ, I do so knowing that He is helping because He is an actively living being. We can feel His presence among us; He will help us! But we have to learn His language, and His language today is that of spiritual science. That is the way it is for the present. And we have to find the courage to represent and support this spiritual science as much as we can among ourselves and before others.

This summer, let us reflect upon this and let us meditate on it until we meet again.

# NOTES

## 1 The Immortality of the I

1 This comment refers to the lecture cycle *Gegenwärtiges und Vergangenes im Menschengeist*, lectures February 13 to May 30, 1916; vol. 167 in the Collected Works, (Dornach, Switzerland: Rudolf Steiner Verlag, 1962).

2 Johann Christoph Friedrich von Schiller, 1759–1805, German poet, playwright, and critic.
Alexander von Gleichen-Russwurm, 1865–1947, *Kultur-Aberglaube* ("Cultural Superstition"), (Munich: Forum, 1916).

3 Johann Wolfgang von Goethe, 1749–1832, leading German poet. Also wrote extensively on botany, optics, and other scientific topics.

4 Hermann Bahr, 1863–1934, Austrian journalist, playwright, and theater manager. *Expressionismus* ("Expressionism"), 3rd ed., Munich, 1919.

5 Maurice Barrès, 1862–1923, French writer and politician. Boulangist member, Chamber of Deputies (1889–93). Wrote trilogy on his own self-analysis as well as nationalistic works.
Georges-Ernest-Jean-Marie Boulanger, 1837–1891, French general and politician, became figurehead among revanchists, including Bonapartists, royalists, and leftists. Aroused popular enthusiasm among elements antagonistic to government. Fled to England.

6 Karl Kraus, 1874–1936, Austrian satirist, critic, and poet. In his writings attacked middle-class circles and the liberal press. Wrote dramas, essay collections, and translated Shakespeare.

Nikolaus Lenau, pseudonym of Nikolaus Niembsch von Strehlenau, 1802–1850, Austrian poet, born in Hungary. Wrote in tradition of German Romantic pessimism; known for his lyric verse.
Anastasius Grün, pseudonym of Anton Alexander von Auersperg, Duke, 1806–1876. Austrian poet and politician. Outspoken leader of liberal sentiment. Wrote verse and ironic epics.

7 Karl Kraus, *Die demolierte Literatur* ("Literature Demolished"), Vienna, 1896.

8 Goethe, quoted in Bahr, *Expressionismus*, p. 85.

9 Sir Francis Galton, 1822–1911, English scientist. Traveled widely. His studies of meteorology form basis of modern weather maps. Best known for his work in anthropology and the study of heredity; founder of eugenics; devised system of fingerprint identification.

10 Johannes Müller, 1801–1858, German physiologist and comparative anatomist. Taught Virchow, DuBois-Reymond, and Haeckel.

11 Eugène Lévy, *Rudolf Steiners Weltanschauung und ihre Gegner* ("Rudolf Steiner's World View and its Opponents"), Berlin, 1913.

12 Hermann Bahr, *Himmelfahrt* ("Ascension"), Berlin, 1916.

13 Friedrich Wilhelm Ostwald, 1854–1932, German physical chemist. Invented a process for preparation of nitric acid by oxidizing ammonia, important in the production of explosives during World War I. Was awarded 1909 Nobel prize for chemistry.

14 Ulrich von Wilamowitz-Moellendorff, 1848–1931, German scholar. Wrote critical works on Greek history and literature.
Rudolph Christoph Eucken, 1846–1926, German philosopher. Wrote on historical philosophy and his own philosophy of ethical activism. Awarded Nobel prize for literature in 1908.
Josef Kohler, 1849–1919, German jurist and writer.

15 Gustav von Schmoller, 1838–1917, German economist.
Lujo Brentano, 1844–1931, German economist. A leading pacifist

and opponent of German militarism. Awarded Nobel prize for peace in 1927.

16 Charles-Robert Richet, 1850–1935, French physiologist. Conducted research in serum therapy, epilepsy; discovered phenomenon of anaphylaxis. Awarded 1913 Nobel prize for physiology. Also studied psychic phenomena.

17 Sigmund Freud, 1856–1939, Austrian neurologist and founder of psychoanalysis.

18 Rudolf Steiner, *Theosophy: An Introduction to the Supersensible Knowledge of the World and the Destination of Man*, (Hudson, NY: Anthroposophic Press, 1988).

19 Herman Grimm, *Goethe*, vol. 2, Lecture 23, p. 171f., Berlin, 1817.

20 Thomas Henry Huxley, 1825–1895, English biologist. Foremost advocate in England of Darwin's theory of evolution. Engaged Bishop Samuel Wilberforce (1805–1873) in famous exchange at Oxford (1860). In later years wrote philosophy.

21 Richard Wahle, *Die Tragikomödie der Weisheit: Die Ergebnisse und die Geschichte des Philosophierens* ("The Tragicomedy of Wisdom: The Results and History of Philosophy"), Vienna and Leipzig, 1915, p. 132.

## 2 Blood and Nerves

1 These names do not refer to present-day planets but to ancient evolutionary stages and are therefore capitalized.

2 Rudolf Steiner, *Secrets of the Threshold*, (Hudson, NY: Anthroposophic Press, 1987).

3 Rudolf Steiner, *The Gospel of St. Luke*, 3rd ed., (London: Rudolf Steiner Press, 1988).

4 Rudolf Steiner, *Vom Menschenrätsel* ("The Riddle of Man"), vol. 20 in the Collected Works, (Dornach, Switzerland: Rudolf Steiner Verlag, 1984).

5 Johann Christoph Friedrich von Schiller, 1759–1805, German poet, playwright, and critic. Wrote *Letters on the Aesthetic Education of Man* (1795).

6 Heinrich Deinhardt, often mentioned by Steiner. No biographical information available. His *Beiträge zur Würdigung Schillers* ("Contributions to the Appreciation of Schiller") were reissued in 1922 in Stuttgart.

7 Johann Gottlieb Fichte, 1762–1814, German philosopher.
Friedrich Wilhelm Joseph von Schelling, 1775–1854, German philosopher. Leading figure of German idealism. Clashed with Fichte and later also with Hegel. Wrote on Transcendental Idealism.
Georg Wilhelm Friedrich Hegel, 1770–1831, German philosopher. Last of the great German Idealist system-building philosophers. Created monistic system reconciling opposites by means of dialectic process. Viewed history as similar process, dialectic of thesis and its implied antithesis leading to synthesis. Exerted influence on Existentialists, Positivists, and Marx.
Immanuel Hermann von Fichte, 1796–1879, son of Johann Gottlieb. Philosopher, exponent of an ethical or speculative theism.

8 Ralph Waldo Trine, American spiritualistic writer.

9 Rudolf Steiner, *Die Aufgabe der Geisteswissenschaft und deren Bau in Dornach* ("The Mission of Spiritual Science and its Building in Dornach"), Berlin, 1916.

10 Adolphe Pégoud, 1889–1915, French aviator. Known for acrobatic flying feats; credited with first "looping the loop" in an aircraft. Killed in aerial combat.

11 Johann Wolfgang von Goethe, 1749–1832, German poet and playwright. *Faust* (1808–32), a drama in verse, is his masterpiece.

12 Oskar Blumenthal, 1852–1917, German playwright and critic.

13 It was not possible to ascertain the identity of the person Steiner refers to here.

## 3 THE TWELVE HUMAN SENSES

1 Helmuth Johannes Ludwig von Moltke, 1848–1916, German soldier. Chief of general staff (from 1906) and director of German strategy at beginning of World War I (1914). Lost the first battle of the Marne (Sept. 1914) and was relieved of his command (Nov. 1914).

2 Eduard von Hartmann, 1842–1906, German philosopher. *Grundriss der Psychologie* ("Basic Psychology"), Bad Sachsa, 1908.

3 Rudolf Steiner, *An Outline of Occult Science*, 3rd ed., repr., (Spring Valley, NY: Anthroposophic Press, 1989).

4 Jakim and Boaz are the words inscribed on the two columns at the front of Solomon's Temple. See the Old Testament, I Kings, Chapter 7; II Chronicles, Chapter 3. See also Rudolf Steiner, *Bilder Okkulter Siegel und Säulen* ("Pictures of Occult Seals and Pillars"), vol. 284/285 in the Collected Works (Dornach, Switzerland: Rudolf Steiner Verlag, 1977).

5 Leo Nikolayevich Tolstoy, Count, 1828–1910. Russian novelist and moral philosopher.

6 John Ernst Worrell Keely, 1827–1898. Claimed invention of a perpetual-motion system (1873). After his death, his apparatus was proven a fraud.

7 Hermann Bahr, *Himmelfahrt* ("Ascension"), Berlin, 1916.

8 Hermann Bahr, *Himmelfahrt* and see Lecture One, notes 13–17.

9 Council of Trent, council of the Roman Catholic Church, 1545–1563.

10 Richard M. Meyer, 1860–1914, German philologist.

11 Franz Ferdinand, 1863–1914, Archduke of Austria. Nephew of Emperor Franz Joseph and heir to crown. Was assassinated with his wife on June 28, 1914, by a Serbian nationalist at Sarajevo, Bosnia. This assassination led to World War I.

12 Rudolf Steiner, *Die Aufgabe der Geisteswissenschaft und deren Bau in Dornach* ("The Mission of Spiritual Science and its Building in Dornach"), Berlin, 1916.

13 Immanuel Hermann von Fichte, 1796–1879, son of Johann Gottlieb. Philosopher, exponent of an ethical or speculative theism.

14 Helena Petrovna Blavatsky, 1831–1891, American theosophist. Organized Theosophical Society in 1875 with Henry Steel Olcott. Annie Besant, 1847–1933, English theosophist and Indian political leader.

15 Franz Hartmann, 1838–1912, doctor and theosophist. Founded his own movement within theosophy.

### 4 The Human Organism through the Incarnations

1 Sandro Botticelli, 1445–1510, Italian painter.

2 Karl Langer, 1819–1887, German anatomist.
Franz Peter Schubert, 1797–1828, Austrian composer. Famous for his song cycles.
Franz Joseph Haydn, 1732–1809, Austrian composer. Regarded as first great master of the symphony and the quartet.
Ludwig van Beethoven, 1770–1827, German composer. Studied with Haydn.

3 Hermann Schaaffhausen, 1816–1893, German anthropologist.

4 Rudolf Steiner, *Knowledge of the Higher Worlds and Its Attainment*, 3rd ed., (Hudson, NY: Anthroposophic Press, 1986).

5 Hans Vaihinger, 1852–1933, German philosopher. Developed his "As if" philosophy 1911.

6 Rudolf Steiner, *Vom Menschenrätsel* ("The Riddle of Man"), vol. 20 in the Collected Works, (Dornach, Switzerland: Rudolf Steiner Verlag, 1984).

## 5 BALANCE IN LIFE

1 Alfred Kerr, real name Kempner, 1867–1948, German theater critic. He was a relative of Friederike Kempner (1836–1904), a poet notorious for the unintended humor of her poems.

2 Fritz Mauthner, 1849–1923, German writer and theater critic. Exponent of philosophical Skepticism.

3 Fritz Mauthner, *Beiträge zu einer Kritik der Sprache* ("Contributions to a Critique of Language"), 3 vols., 1901–2; *Wörterbuch der Philosophie* ("Dictionary of Philosophy"), 2 vols., 1910–11.

4 Friedrich Karl Christian Ludwig Büchner, 1824–1899, German physician and philosopher. Evolved philosophy of consistent, determinist materialism; roused controversy with view of mind and consciousness as epiphenoma of physical brain.
David Friedrich Strauss, 1808–1874, German theologian and philosopher.
Carl von Voit, 1831–1908, German physiologist. Conducted pioneering research on animal and human metabolism.

## 6 THE FEELING FOR TRUTH

1 Rudolf Steiner, *Twelve Moods*, (Spring Valley, NY: Mercury Press, 1984).

2 Oskar Simony, 1852–1915, Austrian mathematician.

3 Rudolf, 1858–1889, Archduke and Crown Prince of Austria. Only son of Emperor Franz Joseph. Died, allegedly by suicide, at his hunting lodge Mayerling together with Baroness Maria Vetsera.

4 Oskar Simony, *Gemeinverständliche, leicht controlierbare Lösung der Aufgabe: In ein ringförmiges geschlossenes Band einen Knoten zu machen, und verwandter merkwürdiger Probleme* ("Generally understandable and controllable solution to the problem of making a knot in a ringlike, closed ribbon, and other curious related problems"), 3rd. ed., Vienna, 1881.

5 Robert Hamerling, pseudonym of Rupert Hammerling, 1830–1889, Austrian poet. Best known for his epics *Ahasverus in Rom* (1865) and *Homunculus* (1888).

6 Arnold Böcklin, 1827–1901, Swiss painter. Known for paintings of moody landscapes and sinister allegories.
Fritz von Uhde, 1848–1911, German painter.
Adolph Friedrich Erdmann von Menzel, 1815–1905, German painter.
Carl Spitzweg, 1808–1885, German painter. Most representative of Biedermeier artists in Germany. Known for humorous and detailed portraits of small-town characters.

7 Franz von Lenbach, 1836–1904, German painter. His works included copies of Rubens, Titian, and others, as well as portraits of famous people.

8 Antoine Joseph Wiertz, 1806–1865, painter.

9 Peter Paul Rubens, 1577–1640, Flemish painter. Renowned for excellence of his coloring.

10 Leonardo da Vinci, 1452–1519, Italian painter, sculptor, architect, engineer, and scientist.

11 Michelangelo, 1475–1564, Italian sculptor, painter, architect, and poet.

12 Herman Grimm, *Goethe*, vol. 2, Lecture 23, p. 171f., Berlin, 1817.
Rudolph Christoph Eucken, 1846–1926, German philosopher. See Lecture One, note 14.
Josef Kohler, 1849–1919, German jurist and writer. See Lecture One, note 14.
Georg Simmel, 1858–1918, German philosopher and sociologist. His work was very influential in establishing sociology as a scientific discipline in the United States.

13 Richard M. Meyer, 1860–1914, German philologist.

14 *J'accuse von einem Deutschen* ("J'accuse by a German"), Lausanne, 1915.

15 Franz Oppenheimer, 1864–1943, German economist and sociologist. The reply was *J'accuse! Aus den Aufzeichnungen eines feldgrauen Akademikers* (J'accuse! From the Notes of an Academic in field-gray"), Berlin, 1915.

16 Francis Bacon, 1st Baron Verulam and Viscount St. Albans, 1561–1626. English philosopher and author.
William Shakespeare, 1564–1616, English dramatist and poet.
Jakob Böhme, 1575–1624. German mystic. He was first a shoemaker, then had a mystical experience in 1600.

17 Rudolf Steiner, *Vom Menschenrätsel* ("The Riddle of Man"), vol. 20 in the Collected Works, (Dornach, Switzerland: Rudolf Steiner Verlag, 1984).

## 7 TOWARD IMAGINATION

1 See Lecture Two, note 4.

2 William Shakespeare, *The Merchant of Venice*, Act 5, Scene 1.

3 Franz Hartmann, 1838–1912, doctor and theosophist. Founded his own movement within theosophy.

4 Translator's note: The Latin word *bonus* means "good."

5 James I, 1566–1625, King of Scotland as James VI and of Great Britain as James I. Son of Mary, Queen of Scots. Succeeded to English throne at death of Queen Elizabeth in 1603. During his reign group of scholars prepared new version of the Bible in English, called in his honor King James Bible (1611).

6 Francisco Suarez, 1548–1617, Spanish theologian and scholastic philosopher. Joined Society of Jesus (1564), considered foremost Jesuit theologian.

7 Ignatius of Loyola, 1491–1556, Spanish religious. Founded Society of Jesus in 1539. Began composition of his *Spiritual Exercises* in 1523.

8 Rudolf Steiner, *The Riddles of Philosophy*, (Spring Valley, NY: Anthroposophic Press, 1973).

Urbaine-Jean-Joseph Leverrier, 1811–1877, French astronomer. Investigated disturbance in the motion of Uranus (1845), making calculations indicating the presence of an unknown planet, which was discovered in 1846 and named Neptune.

9 Rudolf Steiner, *An Outline of Occult Science*, 3rd ed., repr., (Spring Valley, NY: Anthroposophic Press, 1989).

10 After these words, Rudolf Steiner spoke about the day care nursery the members of the Anthroposophical Society in Berlin had organized:
"I would like to add here that our dear friends who organized and cared so devotedly for our day care nursery are concerned that it might be forgotten—not completely of course, but perhaps almost forgotten. Naturally, we will have a kind of vacation, but after that the nursery will have to open again. Then we will need some money and, above all, some dear friends who will help with the day care—of course, only those who can help. Maybe there are women here who could help with the cooking or something like that. All this is needed. Those who have worked in the nursery and know something about such matters can tell you that its results are very good. The children gained something from having come here; something has been made of them. Therefore, I would like to ask that the women who could take on this task again do so as a labor of love. Of course, if you take on such a task, you have to stay with it. If you cannot make a certain commitment to it, it is better not to take it on. For example, we cannot have somebody promising to be in the nursery at 5 o'clock and then send a note in the afternoon to cancel; we will not be able to find somebody else to fill in on such short notice. We have to know about cancellations at least one day in advance. Thus, I now ask those friends who can work in the nursery to contact Frau Dannenberg, who, together with others, has done so much for the nursery, so that the nursery can open again in winter."

# Publisher's Note

The lectures printed here were given by Rudolf Steiner to audiences familiar with the general background and terminology of his anthroposophical teaching. It should be remembered that in his autobiography *The Course of My Life,* he emphasizes the distinction between his written works on the one hand, and on the other, reports of lectures that were given as oral communications and were not originally intended for print. For an intelligent appreciation of the lectures it should be borne in mind that certain premises were taken for granted when the words were spoken. "These premises," Rudolf Steiner writes, "include at the very least the anthroposophical knowledge of Man and of the Cosmos in its spiritual essence; also what may be called 'anthroposophical history,' told as an outcome of research into the spiritual world."

